799 k

MW01490753

Stories from my Camino

Kitos Sarthou Olano

Copyright © 2019 by Kitos Sarthou Olano

All rights reserved

ISBN - 978-1-7340662-0-3

I gratefully acknowledge the CAMINO GUIDES *A Pilgrim's Guide to the Camino de Santiago Camino Frances St. Jean Pied de Port - Santiago de Compostela* for permission to reprint the cover of the guide on page 45.

To Les, for all our live's journeys.

To Mama, for all the travel you wanted to do but couldn't.
I take you with me in all of mine.

Introduction

When does one decide to walk the Camino? And more importantly, why does one walk the Camino? How does one even learn about it, given that it's not widely advertised in travel brochures. And what is the Camino?

There are many resources online about the Camino de Santiago, or the Way of Saint James so I will not go into a lot of detail about it. Here's what I learned from conversations with people on the Way, as well as Wikipedia[1]: the Camino can start from different points in Europe but they all lead to the cathedral of the apostle Saint James the Great in Santiago de Compostela in Galicia, where tradition has it that his remains are buried. During the middle ages, the pilgrimage started from one's home, but today, there are several popular staging points. The most popular is the Camino Frances which starts in Saint Jean Pied de Port at the foot of the Pyrenees and is the route that we took. During the Middle Ages, this pilgrimage was one of the most important Christian pilgrimages, along with those to Rome and Jerusalem. Back then, the main routes were highly travelled but because of the Black Death, the Protestant Reformation and political unrest, it lost its popularity by the 16th century. In the 1980s, there were only a few hundred pilgrims registering at the pilgrim's office in Santiago. However, starting in the early 1990s, a few thousand pilgrims started walking the Way and by 2000, there were over 50,000 (with spikes during the Holy Years - the years when the July 25 Feast of Saint James falls on a Sunday). The last Holy Year was 2010 which saw over 270,000 pilgrims and in 2017, the year that we walked, the number of pilgrims registering at the cathedral hit the 300,000 mark for the first time. The next Holy Year is 2021. Pilgrims traditionally walked the Camino for indulgences or penance, but in the modern era, it's more about spirituality, travel and sightseeing, or taking a break from fast-paced modern life.

Retirement was quickly looming on the horizon for me. I had worked for the company for over 30 years but did not climb the corporate ladder much. My first role lasted 25 years (with increasing responsibility, as they say) which made me a sort of resident expert in a small niche, and my second role, which I did for the last five years, was not what I expected it to be. The more senior people who I wanted to work with in that group retired soon after I moved into it, leaving me with a group of much younger co-workers as well as a very young manager. I loved

---

[1] Wikipedia contributors. "Camino de Santiago." *Wikipedia, The Free Encyclopedia*. Wikipedia, The Free Encyclopedia, 19 Jul. 2019. Web. 23 Jul. 2019.

the work but quickly realized that I got into it late in the game. The young ones were much, much better than me. They got the prime projects, eventually leaving me with the dregs, like office relocation and scheduling training classes. I was truly happy for my younger coworkers but at the same time, my ego and self-worth took a beating. Thank goodness that by that point, I was financially able to retire! I figured that I fought the good fight for over 30 years, and it was time to do something else. But what was that something else? I had some idea of what I wanted to do, but felt like I needed substantial quiet time to reflect and as corny as this sounds, listen to what God had planned for me. I also needed to do something big to restore my self-worth and confidence.

The Camino seemed to be the answer for both my goals. The more I thought about it, the more I was convinced that we should do our Camino as soon as we possibly could. My husband had retired a couple of years before me and we were facing the challenge of potentially being with each other 24/7 after my own retirement. What better way to test this than by actually being together 24/7 for several weeks?

Here's how I learned about the Camino. I remember having a conversation with one of my brothers more than 25 years ago. He told me about a pilgrimage in Spain where people walk for over 500 miles. When I heard that, I said, why would anyone want to do THAT? This conversation remained hidden in the recesses of my mind until I saw the movie The Way [2] and then realized that was the pilgrimage my brother was talking about. I was mesmerized by the film, and thought, maybe someday, but not now. Right now I'm working and putting kids through college. But when my retirement was imminent, it seemed to be the right time to make the dream a reality.

As soon as I knew my last day of work, I bought our tickets to Spain and Les and I started doing baby hikes. We hit the Bay Area trails and walked for a few miles each time. We started researching and shopping which took the form of watching different movies about the Camino and videos upon videos on YouTube. We would watch the videos and say, what's so hard about that? I read blogs and group sites and even went to a pilgrim forum to ask questions. Les's main question was, "what about the bathrooms," which met the reply, "Les, get over it." Our trepidation and excitement was increasing every day, with excitement winning out and by the time we left, we were super excited and felt as ready as we could possibly be!

A note about Les's name: he has many nicknames: from a family nickname (Boyet, or little boy, as he was the second son) to a school one (Ach, short for Achilles, which is his real name) and an Americanized one (Les, which I jokingly refer to as his Anglo name). For the purpose of this book, I am using Les because it's the name he used on the Camino. What can I say, we're Filipino and we have many nicknames.

---

[2] *The Way*. Directed by Emilio Estevez. Spain: Elixir Films, 2010

For those we met on the Camino who gave me permission to use their first names and pictures, I did just that, while for those whose contact information I did not have, or who are now deceased, I changed their names and pixelated their faces in the pictures.

This book is written in a chronological sequence, from October 3 to November. 14, 2017. Each day happens as how a day typically happens, with no profound lessons or aha moments. How could there be? Aside from the six to eight hours of daily walking, we were too busy washing our clothes, taking care of our feet to prevent blisters, figuring out where we were staying the next day and, most importantly, finding the restaurant with the best pilgrim meal. It was at the end of the journey, and especially when I was writing this, that the true lessons were revealed. But oh what glorious lessons they were! We met many pilgrims who were on their second, third or even seventh Camino. At first I could not understand why the heck would anyone want to do THAT? But now I know, and I would like to do it again. Enjoy my journey.

Last note: I will be using "my" a lot, instead of "our." While Les and I went on this journey together, we each had our own Caminos; he has his story, and this one's mine.

Day 1 minus 2

We're Off to Spain!

When does one's Camino start? The traditional answer is that it begins as soon as you leave your house because back in the day, many centuries ago, pilgrims just stepped out of their front doors and began walking. The modern answer is that it begins at the airport. My deep answer is that my Camino started when I was born. I feel as if everything that has happened in my life has led to my Camino. The modern answer, though, was also true in our case. At the Oakland airport, while we were waiting at the terminal for our flight, an older lady with a Camino badge on her backpack walked by, looking for something. Les noticed her and pointed out her backpack to me and a few minutes later, she came over and asked us about our flight. That's how we started talking and she confirmed that indeed, she had done the Camino and gave us practical tips about it. Her name was Marilyn and she was very nice, and very excited for us. She was jealous that we were at the excited-for-the-Camino-to-start stage because everything wonderful was ahead of us. She gave us her email address and made us promise to tell her all about our journey. Les said later that meeting her was a sign that our Camino was underway.

We took a British Airways flight from Oakland to London to Barcelona and arrived Oct 4. The trip was uneventful, which is how we like our flights. We had a few hours' layover in Gatwick where we had lunch and I resisted buying souvenirs which I would have had to carry around for weeks. At least we saw where to buy cookies that our daughter wanted. We could buy them for her on our return trip, which felt oh so distant to me.

We arrived safely in Barcelona and then felt totally unsafe on the cab ride to the hotel. The cab driver drove so fast! We noticed that a lot of apartment balconies had flags - some had the Spanish flag but more displayed the Catalan flag. The Catalonians had been in the news recently for their secessionist push. Barcelona was ground zero for the movement as it was the capital of Catalonian country. In fact, there were demonstrations every weekend and they were loud and boisterous. We asked the taxi driver if Barcelona was safe (so American!) and he said not to worry, as no one wanted to risk endangering the tourists.

We stayed at Hotel Expo in Barcelona. I picked it for its proximity to the train station, where we had an early ride the next day to Pamplona. After checking in, we went to the station to familiarize ourselves with the layout and the process of checking in because if we missed this train, we would also miss the bus connection to Saint Jean Pied de Port. We meticulously planned everything!

That evening we walked up and down the main street but decided not to go downtown as we were tired from the flight. The tapas place that I wanted to try was a 20-minute walk but we would save that for after the Camino. When we did loop back to Barcelona a month and a half later, we went to the tapas place on our last night, but it was closed. Travel lesson #1: when you are abroad and you want to eat somewhere or do something, don't wait.

Instead, we had dinner at the rooftop garden of our hotel. We had Spanish wine that came in a white bottle with red polka dots and burgers! Really, our first night in Barcelona, we had burgers. But they were delicious and unlike the burgers in the States (even though they were advertised as American-style burgers) so we were both happy. I guess when you're eating burgers abroad, they just taste better not because they are, but because you're in Barcelona, for Pete's sake, and you're enjoying the rooftop garden, the evening breeze, and listening to all the conversations in Spanish. We were at the start of a great adventure!

Day 1 minus 1

Anticipation

We woke up very early and took an early train from Barcelona to Pamplona. Les slept most of the way while I watched the movie Beauty and the Beast in Spanish and arrived in Pamplona during the final fight scene of the movie.

I thought I saw a diagram online that showed that the bus station in Pamplona was within walking distance of the train station, but apparently, it was not true. Fortunately, we met Abby, an American woman who spoke fluent Spanish, and she asked the taxi drivers how far it was. They said it was not walkable. Abby was also walking the Camino, and our first of many Camino angels in Spain. A Camino angel is one who just shows up and helps you exactly when you need it and it is said that the Camino provides them. In fact, there's a saying, "The Camino provides." And this saying is tried, tested and true. Camino angels are not always human. We would learn later that dogs could also be Camino angels. But that's a story for later…

We took a taxi to the bus station where we had lunch. We noticed Basque words on the menu (for example, calamari is called rabas) and noted that the running of the bulls is in June - there were a lot of posters about it. Clearly, it's the biggest thing in Pamplona.

Slowly, we started seeing pilgrims at the bus station. First there were a couple, and the closer it was to the bus's leaving, the more we spotted. They were easy to spot because they all had the trademark backpack and hiking boots.

When the bus finally came, we put our backpacks in the storage compartment underneath it and sat in the first row of seats. While we were waiting for the bus to leave, we saw a young lady arguing with the driver because the driver (who was actually kind of a jerk) would not let her friend get on the bus. The driver eventually did but he gave the guy a bad time because he did not know that he was supposed to put his backpack on the other side of the baggage carrier of the bus. The girl was Fulvia and the guy was Joel, both of whom we would get to know very well over the course of the Camino.

The bus driver continued to be a jerk. At a later bus stop, he did not let a Frenchman get on the bus because he said he did not understand French and could not figure out where the guy wanted to go. I don't speak French either and I could tell he wanted to go to Roncesvalles, which was one of the stops.

On the bus ride, we saw pilgrims walking to Pamplona, on a trail that was coming in and out of the woods. It was very exciting for us to get our first view of pilgrims actually walking. That was going to be us starting tomorrow!

We arrived at St Jean Pied de Port (SJPP) late afternoon and oh my goodness, it was such a beautiful place. So magical with its bridges and narrow medieval cobblestone streets. It looked like a scene right out of a Brothers Grimm (or Disney?) fairy tale. Belle and Gaston would look right at home here, actually.

Our innkeeper was named Jean Claude. He gave us very sage advice and told us to take our time on the Camino and listen to our bodies. He also gave us practical advice such as how to tie our boot laces when we are going up the mountain versus walking in the dessert that is the meseta. He said that going up and down mountains, we need to lace up to the very top of our shoes but on the meseta, we only need to lace up halfway, like low-cut tennis shoes.

The hotel, called Le Chemin ver l'Etoile was in a very old beautiful building with high ceilings. The staircase was in the middle of the building and if you looked straight up, it's a big square. The floor boards were uneven and creaky. Our room had at least eight bunk beds but we were the only ones there. There was only one bunk bed where the bottom part was a double bed, and that's where we slept.

When I went to the bathroom to take a shower, there was a man shaving wearing nothing but a towel. The bathroom was co-ed!!! Ok, I thought, so this is how the Camino was going to be. Each shower stall had a small, and I mean, micro small dressing area and the shower was beyond that. It was just as tiny and my favorite part was that it had an overhead skylight right above my head that let the sunlight in. I loved it!

As we were leaving the hotel to explore the town, we saw Abby and her new friends checking in - Joel, Fulvia and Amanda. Their rooms were on the second floor while ours was on the third floor. Little did we know then that we would cross paths many, many times on the Camino. Especially Joel, with whom we would start and end the Camino.

We had dinner at a small restaurant and had pizza (still in US-food mode) and walked around town, checking in at the Pilgrim office to check the weather in the mountains (highly recommended). It was a go so there's no stopping us now! There were a lot of pilgrims walking around and there was such an excitement, a buzz in the air. Our excitement was building up too. We could not believe that after months of training and planning and watching YouTube videos, we were here. It was about to begin!

At breakfast the next morning, we met a German who just finished walking the Camino. He took the bus back to St Jean and he was on his way back to Germany. It wasn't his first time either! What? You can do it again? Why would anyone want to do THAT!

We also saw Abby who said that the other solo walkers she met (all in their mid 20s/ early 30s) were probably going to sleep in because they were drinking until one in the morning. They did start late, and still overtook us halfway up the mountain, and got to Orrison with plenty of time to do laundry and start with the vino tinto by the time we got there. This was going to be a pattern for the rest of our Camino, and it was established on Day 1.

Day 1: Saint Jean Pied de Port to Orrison

It Begins – Rookie Mistakes and All

We were not off to a good start. Just leaving town, we went the wrong way, because Les said we needed to go right and he was following three Americans (a man and two women) who also went right. I tried to tell him that they said at the Pilgrim Office to go left at the fork in the road. Apparently, he was not listening. After around 100 yards, one of the American ladies stopped and said she thought they were going the wrong way and that we should turn back and go left at the fork. She turned out to be Candy, sister of Craig, who is married to Tina ("the Americans"). We all turned back and saw a group of guys who also told us that if we were going to Orrison, we should have turned left at the fork. Now Les believed me. And with that, drum roll please, we re-started our journey.

Two feet outside of town, the road up the Pyrenees got real steep real fast. We were still jet-lagged, getting used to the altitude and walking with a full backpack - we were in trouble! Well, just me, not Les. He was doing well, walking ahead of me and I was just…slow! The whole morning was a struggle, and when we had to get off the road and walk on a path, it was muddy and cold and miserable. But the views, oh the views! The views kept getting better the higher we walked. It was all worth it.

Also, on our first day, we made the biggest rookie mistake that we could ever make: we did not have enough water, just a small bottle between the two of us. And we knew we did not have enough water but left anyway because all the shops in town were still closed and all the pilgrims were already leaving and we were anxious to leave too so we left with one small bottle between the two of us. I figured, it was only six kms today. Easy peasy. It should be enough, we kept telling ourselves. However, we ran out of water halfway through so when we got to the albergue (pilgrim hostel in Spanish), Les's hands were cramped around his walking sticks and I was nauseated and ready to pass out.

There's only one albergue or pilgrim hostel in Orrison, the Auberge (pilgrim hostel, in French) Orrison. The bar was on the main level and the sleeping quarters were behind it. For purposes of this narrative, when I say "bar," I mean the bar/restaurant. In Spain, a "bar" bears no negative connotation, unlike in the US where it conjures seedy little places and pick-up joints. Here, everyone goes to the bar - it's not uncommon to see multi-generational families hanging out in a bar. It's just what Spanish people do before their three-hour dinners. Every night.

In any case, by the time we arrived in Orrison, Les's hands were cramping so hard that his hands could not un-grip his walking sticks and I was ready to pass out. As soon as we walked into the bar, I ordered two glasses of orange juice, which we chugged then I ordered two Cokes, which we also chugged (note on Coke: here, it's made with real sugar, like Mexican and Philippine Coke we grew up with so it tastes better and more refreshing than what we have in the States, where corn syrup is used). Les and I started to feel better, and we ordered a cafe con leche for slower sipping. It was around 2 PM and dinner was at 7 so we had five hours to kill. Les sat and started drinking vino tinto with a Frenchman, Roger, who we chatted with as he was overtaking us on the way here. Remember the phrase vino tinto or red wine, as you will see this phrase throughout this narrative. In the meantime, I checked in and got situated. When I got back to the bar, Les was surrounded by a few people, drinking and chatting away. We met half the people at the albergue in the course of the afternoon over snacks, cafe con leche (coffee with milk) and wine.

Dinner was very interesting. After the meal, each of us was asked to get up in front of everyone and share why we were doing the Camino. I said that I had recently retired and was looking for guidance for the next phase of my life. Les said, because my wife said. Everyone laughed and the rest of the night, we socialized with the other pilgrims. Good thing we did or we would not have known to order lunch for the next day's walk as there were no towns between Orrison and Roncesvalles, the next day's stop.

Here are the people we met that night and the countries they were from: Joel (CAN), Abby (US), Fulvia (BRA), Amanda (US), Maggie (AUS), Jill (AUS), Femi (SUI), Peter (ENG), Boris (GER), Roger (FRA), Candy, Craig and Tina (US). We also saw a Korean family: the parents and two children, a girl who was around 12 years old and a boy who was 6. We later learned that the parents' backpacks were so heavy as they not only contained their children's clothes but also a rice cooker, which the mom would use a lot on the Camino. Originally from South Korea, they now lived in Australia. They both quit their jobs because the dad said it was his calling to do the Camino but the mom was always stressed out about the budget.

When we got to Orrison, the fog was so thick that we could not see the valley floor below. It lifted in the afternoon and we were able to take lots of pictures of the beautiful view. We were also treated to the sight of a noisy herd of sheep walking through town. There were hundreds of them, a lot wearing bells around their necks, and shepherds prodding them along. What a sight and sound! I was lucky to be able to capture a few seconds of video of the cacophony on my phone.

The bathroom was also interesting in this place. We were given two tokens and each token got you FIVE minutes of shower time. It took me forever to figure out how to use the tokens, but when I did, I managed to enjoy a hot, albeit quick, shower on a cold night.

Since many people arrived before us, Les and I both had upper bunks. Les was furious when he learned about this. He threw a hissy fit and said that there was no way he was going to sleep on a top bunk and that he would rather sleep on the bench outside the sleeping quarters. I thought, really, this is only the first day and we were already arguing? I finally told him that the owners would never allow him to sleep outdoors. We were in the mountains (hello!) and he would freeze to death. He finally acquiesced and slept on the top bunk at the end of the room that had seven bunk beds. Because we drank so much wine that day, we both had to go to the bathroom that night - me, twice and he, five times (or so he said). We could not turn on the lights so as not to disturb the other pilgrims. Les, when he did sleep, snored loudly and I just hoped everyone had good ear plugs on!

Day 2 Orrison to Roncesvalles

More Pyrenees

After getting our sandwiches for the day, we proceeded to climb the Pyrenees some more, around four more hours hiking up. Oh lord, it was so so hard! We saw a food truck on the way up and right away, I gave the vendor my brand new blanket to lighten my load. I had been waffling about whether I would bring it or not anyway because the albergues provided blankets so losing it was just fine with me.

At the top of the Pyrenees, we crossed the border into Spain and there was an unexpected cell tower at the top of the mountain that was supposed to be used in emergencies. Someone told me later that it did not work. I don't know about that, but I certainly hope it's not true in case someone really needed the service. It was here that we saw our first group of biker pilgrims. I could not imagine how they were able to go up the mountains on their bikes, especially at the steep inclines.

Les and I took the "suave" or "easier" path down, which added 5 kms to our hike. I couldn't believe how slow I was walking, even coming down. We walked five hours going down and I honestly thought we were lost because it took us so long to get to Roncesvalles. Towards the end, when we had no more food, I started eating pinches of salt from the little plastic bag of salt that was in my pocket to keep my energy up. I read that it was advisable to do this in case of emergency and to fight dehydration. Little did I know that the emergency would come on day 2! I was actually feeling so inadequate - first, we did not have enough water on day 1 and then today, we ran out of food. I hoped that we would learn from these mistakes quickly because we had a long way to go!

Even though the hike was very difficult, we had the most amazing views. The higher we got, the more amazing the views became. We passed the first of many, many Marian grottoes. There were also stone huts for the pilgrims and I guess the shepherds too, to take shelter when the weather got really bad and it would not be advisable to walk further. A lot of people have died in these mountains, as evidenced by the crosses and markers we started to see at the side of the road. We heard that one of the biggest causes of death is inclement weather, which result in pilgrims falling off cliffs in these mountains. Other causes of death were health reasons (heart attacks, dehydration) and also vehicular accidents, when the paths were right next to the highways. It doesn't help that a lot of Spaniards drive fast and furious.

We saw lots of animals: sheep with bells, horses and cows with bells, even pigs with bells. There was no fog for the most part but it did come and go. We could see it coming, then enveloping us, cutting visibility to no more than a few feet, then it would leave, and everything was clear again.

As we were nearing Roncesvalles, Les had an incident with a herd of wild horses: one of the horses galloped past him, then stopped in front of him and turned around to look at him because he thought that Les was gonna mess with his mom but the horse's dad must have motioned to him that Les was ok so the horse galloped away. Les said he was ready to poke the horse's eyes out with his walking sticks as those were the only weapons he had. It's a good thing it did not come to that! I was not there to witness it, but this is how Les tells the story and he's been sticking to it. He was unnerved by what happened to him though, so it must have happened the way he said it did.

In Roncesvalles, we saw Abby at an outdoor restaurant in front of an albergue. She was happy to see us and she and the others were starting to worry because it took us so long to get there! She told us to go ahead and check in at the albergue (we had reservations at a fancy hotel called Casa de los Beneficiados but I didn't tell her that) and they'd meet us afterwards. We checked in to our hotel which was built in 1741 and where Charlemagne allegedly stayed - I was looking for graffiti that said "Charlie slept here" but there was none. I didn't want to leave the room because it was so nice and my legs were numb, but we went back to albergue by which time Abby and company had gone to Mass. The only person we knew was Jill from Australia, and we had sangria and chips with her. I asked Les to order at the bar and the only word he knew in Spanish was sangria so that's what we drank, even though he really wanted wine. He would eventually learn the words vino and tinto.

We had a proper dinner at the hotel, where we ordered more rabas, had our laundry done, slept soundly and the next morning, had a buffet breakfast (we took a few pieces of bread to go). The food was delicious and our room was big and comfortable and we had our own bathroom.

Day 3 Roncesvalles to Zubiri

A Russian in Spain

Met Patata, the Italian Shaman at the famous signpost that said Santiago de Compostela was 790 kms away. We never found out his name, just that he dressed like a hippie from the 70s and looked like Christ with his beard. We called him Patata because when we asked him to take our picture at the signpost, instead of asking us to smile, he yelled out, patata! We laughed out loud and looked so happy in our pictures. We learned later that he and his friend traveled with hardly any money, which is the closest to a medieval pilgrim as one could get. You see, back in those days, pilgrims had only the clothes on their back and relied on the kindness of the locals to feed and shelter them. In any case, we saw Patata and his friend panhandling a couple of times for their dinner and donativo (albergues that would take donations based only on

what the pilgrim can afford) and we would give them all our change and even some food. He was very thankful every time we helped him out.

Today was a beautiful walk through forests and storybook medieval towns. The doors of the houses were so old, so solid, so beautiful with lots of interesting doorways, with plants and planter boxes.

We thought the first two days were the hardest but this was very difficult as well. We had to walk for a long time down a wide path of rocks which was very difficult because they were loose.

We stopped at a restaurant for lunch and had our first taste of Spanish time, meaning in Spain, time is relative and there is never ever a sense of urgency. Les ordered the pasta, which the guy said would take 20 minutes to prepare, but it took an hour. Les was still very impatient at this point and we were at that restaurant for an hour and a half. We saw the Americans there and had a drink with them but they headed out shortly after.

Yesterday Les had a horse incident. Today, he had a dog incident. We were walking on the path with big rocks and he flew by me, running fast. He said that there was a dog following us but every time Les looked at him, the dog would stop and look behind him. It was the funniest thing! Les was afraid of the dog (of all dogs, really, because of a childhood incident where dogs mauled him) because it was SO big (slightly bigger than my Simon, who's 23 pounds). He said the dog was following us because we had food in my backpack. I thought the dog looked really friendly and harmless. After about 20 minutes, the dog stopped following us but we could see him alongside us, shadowing us on a parallel path. After a few minutes, he disappeared completely. We did not know it then but there are very friendly Camino dogs who walk with people and guide them on the way. We now believe that he was a Camino dog and he just wanted to walk with us!

In Zubiri, we stayed at Suseia Albergue, which was a couple of kms from the bridge that we crossed to get into town. There were plenty of albergues near the bridge so it was a bummer that we had to walk more to get to ours. We were totally out of gas when we walked into town and it was starting to get dark too. Our albergue, though, was very highly rated and when we got there, we found out why.

Aleks (short for Aleksei), a Russian immigrant who runs the albergue, was a friendly young man and was very solicitous of our needs. He said that we were the last to arrive (not surprisingly) and asked if we wanted to order dinner for 10 euros each. Of course we said yes! That night, he cooked a 5-course dinner. It was delicious and artsy too: salad with quinoa, broth, a chorizo on top of a slice of bread, egg and rice embotido with tomato sauce, lemon yogurt with shaved chocolate, and finally, chocolate truffles for dessert. Lots of wine and bread as well. After dinner, we had a nice conversation with him where he told us that he moved from Russia to Spain when he was very young and that he enjoyed the opportunities he had in Spain. In fact, he said he saved and saved and saved and now he owned his own albergue! His experience definitely resonated with us, being immigrants to the US. We could definitely relate to his struggle and were happy for his success.

Peter (AUS) was staying at the same albergue. He was a really nice fellow and we chatted for a bit. Peter just finished the Camino, took the bus back to SJPP and was starting again. He first walked during the summer and this time, he wanted to walk in the fall. We couldn't believe it. He was the second person we met who was doing that; Roger being the first one.

We met an Australian couple who were very nice; he had just booked the next place to stay, but she was very worried about their budget. The husband kept telling her not to worry because everything was going to be all right. We later learned from other pilgrims that they did not finish because they really struggled with the physical aspect of the Camino. Come to think of it, they both seemed overweight and out of shape. I hope they get to finish it someday.

We also met a lovely young Irish couple from Dublin. She was a chef and we did not find out what the guy did, but he was very proud of her being a chef. They told us about the albergue in Roncesvalles that we did not stay in. He said that it had around 300 beds. There were some dividers which did not quite reach the ceiling so they heard everything: people going in and out of the bathrooms all night so it was hard to sleep. Glad we stayed at the hotel! Les was amused that the girl went down to breakfast the next morning wearing her pajamas while everyone else was already dressed and ready to start walking. We did not see this couple again but then again, they were only walking for a week.

We also met two friendly Spanish guys from Santander who were walking for just a week because they had to go back to work the next week. Apparently, it's common for Spaniards to go on the Camino a week at a time during their annual vacation. The two guys did not join us for dinner. Instead, they each had a bocadillo (a meat sandwich, usually on a French roll) for dinner - we found out soon after that those sandwiches were very cheap - around 3 euros each. One of the guys spoke very good English while the other one, none at all but we had fun chatting with them.

We were in a bedroom with three bunk beds and Les and I both had top bunks. Because I didn't want a repeat of the first night, I asked the Spanish group we were sharing the room with if they were ok with us taking down the mattress so Les could sleep on the floor as he had a hard time going up and down bunk beds. They said no problem. The Spaniards were so nice; one of the ladies showed us the closet for the extra blankets which she told me to take if we decided to sleep downstairs.

We asked Aleks if we could sleep in the living/dining room and he said it was fine with him (he was a real sweetheart of a kid) so Les slept on the sofa and I slept on the recliner.

Aleks set up the breakfast food on the table before he went home. Because Les hardly had wine with dinner, (he thought that we were going to sleep on top bunks), he finally had wine and we snacked on the breakfast food (just a little) before going to bed.

Day 4 Zubiri to Pamplona

Camino Angel or Ghost?

This was a very long day - 20.9 kms. The trail was wide but had lots and lots of large rocks on the way down so we were slow.

We had a snack mid-morning and saw the Spaniards who were in the albergue the night before and I talked to the two couples for a while. One of the guys (Jose) asked me why Les and I were carrying our backpacks. We were already big, and our backpacks were also big. He told us that they were using a courier service called caminofacil.net No wonder they only had day packs! They were just carrying water and some food. At the same cafe, Patata the shaman was also taking a break and when Les told him that he had knee problems, he massaged Les's knees with a natural ointment that he kept in a newspaper. I was so touched by his kindness.

It was on this day that we first saw the strange Camino Angel (or ghost as the Americans called him) who we met a few times and he was always walking towards us. He was a squat old man who had a walking stick and looked like a farmer. Les was the one who noticed that we had already come across him earlier. Apparently, he liked walking towards the pilgrims so after walking and meeting pilgrims for a little bit, his wife would drive him further up the trail so the same pilgrims would meet him again. It was freaky to walk the trails and see him walking towards us and then an hour later see him walking towards us again. I don't know what his thing was but I thought it was weird. And let me take back the description of him as a Camino Angel. I don't think he was, as he never really helped anyone. He was just weird.

We also walked by a church in the hills. We went in to talk with the nuns a little bit then a Spanish pilgrim came when we were already outside and ready to leave. He asked us if we went up the steeple. We said that Les's knees were hurting so no. Apparently, the tradition at that church was to ring the bell in the belfry once and he felt he had to do it because his name was the same name as the patron saint of the church. Since we couldn't go up the steeple, he said that he was going to ring the bell hard three times: once for each of us. He said that he was going to pause after each ring so we would hear it. And he did, and we heard it. I thought it was a really sweet gesture on his part.

A few kms before Pamplona, we walked with an American writer who was editing a book (to be published out of Berkeley) and she was taking a lot of pictures: every bench, every street sign, every little detail.

On the outskirts of Pamplona, we saw a painter who was just putting away his art supplies. He was talking to a group of young pilgrims about two paths: one by the river and one through the city which he said was more authentic because it followed the original route more faithfully. Les and I opted for the original route because it was a smidge shorter than the scenic river path.

We walked through the outskirts of the city for an interminable time and when we got to Pamplona, I was so gassed. The route took us across the old bridge, around the castle and through the old town. The narrow cobblestone alleys where they have the running of the bulls were beautiful but I was just too tired to fully appreciate them.

We saw Jill in Pamplona; she told us that she saw Abby and company which made us happy and she also looked up the directions to a restaurant we were interested in going to. At the time, we were using Google maps sparingly even though we had unlimited data with our new carrier. I guess the roaming charges we had with our old carrier when we were in Japan were still fresh in my mind and I did not want to risk a repeat of a $600 phone bill. But I got over that later in the walk. And, as our new carrier promised, we were not charged for roaming. Back to our Camino: we eventually found our hostel called Pension Sarasate at the edge of the old town. The receptionist took a while to attend to us because there was an electrician there that was fixing something…what was it? I don't know. All I know is that she was paying way too much attention to him and I was trying hard not to get too impatient.

The room was very basic but we had our own bathroom so we were happy.

When I removed my backpack, my whole back went numb as did the back of my legs. Right away I thought, where's that website that the Spaniards told us about? That's when we decided to use the courier service that the Spaniards had recommended. Before doing anything else, I set up an online account and arranged for a mochila (backpack) pick-up the next morning. We would do this on a daily basis until October 30, when the courier season ended.

After we showered and changed and washed our undies (our routine for the next few weeks), we went to the town square and saw the Americans and drank beers with them. We also went out for Italian food with them - afterwards Les said, Italian? Really? The food was good though and we ate outdoors. After that, Les and I had pintxos in a small bar. Pintxos is the Basque word for tapas. Here, you don't say tapas; you say pintxos and we were definitely here for the pintxos!

The Americans also told us that they saw Abby strutting in the square; she kept walking up and down the square and they were laughing when they saw that single girl move. And this was just a few minutes before we got there. Unfortunately, we did not see Abby or any of the others in Pamplona.

Day 5 Pamplona to Puente La Reina

Sharing Stories

We were not able to get our credentials stamped anywhere in Pamplona so this morning, we went to a fancy hotel to get it stamped; also because it had a taxi stand and we needed one to get out of town.

We took a taxi to Zariquiegui. When we got there, we saw the French Camino angel/ghost park his car and pointed us in the right direction (ok, I guess he's useful enough). Who exactly is this guy? When we were walking with the Americans later that day (they noticed, and were freaked out by his M.O. too), we saw him again and asked to take a picture with him. The Americans wanted to see if he would show up in the picture which would prove that he was not a ghost. They were so funny! Every time we were with them, we laughed a lot. And of course the non-ghost appeared in the photograph.

The walk up to Alto de Perdon was gradual but long. When we got there, the iconic wrought iron pilgrim representations had Catalonian flags tied to them. Apparently, they were placed there (illegally) the night before by the Catalans. One of the guys we talked to said that he was just waiting for the Guardia Civil to arrive to take them down.

We met a bunch of folks at Alto: A mother and son walking together; Luke, from Holland, who had so many inventions in his head; Virginija from Lithuania who now lives in London. Virginija was having problems with her knee when we met her that day. We hung out with her later on in Santiago and were happy to learn that her knee problem resolved itself and she made it to Santiago without further incident.

The downward trail had a lot of loose stones so we had to be very careful. They were not as big as the ones from Roncesvalles to Zubiri but we had to be careful nonetheless. One wrong step could result in a sprain and the end of the Camino for us. We certainly didn't want that to happen this early in the game, or even later. The goal is to get to Santiago! We also saw Abbey and walked with her for a little bit; an Italian man kinda wanted to walk with her but she wasn't interested. We were starting to realize that with so many young people walking, that Camino romances bloomed and died on these trails.

I also remember walking by a lemonade stand along the way. It was certainly hot enough so I'm sure that stand made money that day.

We stayed at the Hotel Jakue, which turned out to be one of the best hotels we stayed at during the whole Camino. Les and I got a private room with our own bathroom. We loved having an AC because it was a very hot day and we were hot. It was right before we checked out that I saw the recommended maximum setting for the AC, which we totally went over. Oopsies.

There was a part of the hotel that was a true albergue that had bunk beds and a kitchen. In fact, we saw a group of Korean pilgrims in the kitchen preparing dinner. There are a lot of Korean pilgrims because a Korean went on the Camino and wrote a book about his experience. It became a best seller in Korea and made the Camino a popular thing for Korean Christians to do.

After I loaded the laundry, I met the Americans and Les for beer. I love that in Spain, when you ordered drinks, they came with saucers of olives, pickled onions or gherkins. We lost track of time and when I checked on my laundry, it was already done and in fact been unceremoniously dumped on top of the dryer. In folding our clothes, I discovered that I lost a sock which made me sad because they were new. Oh well.

In any case, Tina and Craig told us that the Camino angel/non-ghost was staying at the hotel where we were staying. In fact, we saw him and his wife having a nice dinner at the hotel's restaurant that evening. I couldn't understand how his wife could condone and even support his weird habit but live and let live I guess.

At this point, Les and I had settled into a routine that would last throughout the Camino. As soon as we checked in to a new place, we would take a shower and if there was no washing machine on site, we would wash clothes that needed to be washed, look for a place to dry them: dryers if available, drying racks if provided, window sills, patios, or later when the weather got cold, over radiators. We learned that if our wool socks (which took forever to dry) were still damp, we could dry them by putting them under our bedsheets and our body heat would dry them overnight. If we were using outdoor spaces to dry our clothes, we would take advantage of the last available sliver of sunlight and position our clothes accordingly. We only had a couple of extra shirts and pants and several pairs of socks and undies which worked because a set of clothes could be worn for two, and even up to three days, while undies have to be fresh every day. Whenever we hit a big city, we headed for the local laundry to wash all our clothes, which was just one load. I loved that in Spain, you don't have to put in detergent because the machine does it for you! Small wonders. After taking care of laundry, we would take a nap and later, find a place to unwind and have snacks with a vino tinto, a beer or a shandy, which is a blend of beer and lemonade that was either branded or mixed at the bar and this became my favorite. This drink is not known in the States but I remember having it growing up in Manila at Shakey's pizza so it was delicious as well as a blast from the past. Dinner was usually at 7 and we typically had three to four hours between checking into our lodgings and dinner. The Spaniards actually thought that pilgrims liked to eat at an ungodly early time as they themselves started dinner at 9 and went on through midnight. But they served us dinner "early" anyway, and after the heathens went to bed, then they could have their civilized dinner.

Back to this day…Tina kept getting two new blisters a day. I told her it might be her shoes but she said they had been fine when she was hiking back home. I gave her my extra pair of Injinji's which she gratefully accepted. Injini's are socks that serve as inner liners. They have individual pockets for each toe so there's no friction between toes, hence, no blisters - at least between your toes.

Their stories: Craig was very sick a few months ago and when he got better, he wanted to do the Camino. Tina, his wife, is a nutrition specialist which came in handy as she gave us a lot of nutritional tips for walking. They were both in the military. Candy, Craig's sister, did not talk much and I only discovered her wicked sense of humor after we became friends on social media.

After having drinks with the Americans, Les and I walked around town because I really wanted to see the Puente de la Reina (the Queen's Bridge) - it looked beautiful and graceful in the pictures that I saw of it and in real life, it was even more beautiful. We were lucky enough to get there at sunset so the light was perfect and the reflection of the bridge on the water was perfect too. Les and I have some incredible pictures taken there by Luke who we saw there with a Spanish girl that he met in town.

Walking back to our hotel, we saw Joel having dinner by himself and we invited ourselves to join him for an excellent pilgrim dinner with a lot of wine. Joel is such pleasant company and we had a lot of fun listening to his stories that night. He also said that he was staying further down the road and we told him we were staying next door. He said, the fancy place? We said it was very nice but not really fancy. I guess we did not realize then that the young ones who were walking solo were on a stricter budget and to them, the place we were staying was really fancy. For Les and me, it was about comfort and convenience, and the fact that in our minds, a fifty-dollar hotel room was such a bargain.

Day 6 Puente La Reina to Estella

Filipinos are Donuts and Olano is Basque

The next morning, we had a sumptuous breakfast at the hotel's buffet and took three little bocadillos to go. I was very uncomfortable doing this, for the record. But when we got hungry later that day, I'm glad we did it. Les said everyone does it! And looking around the dining room that morning, I saw that he was right.

We took the bus from Puente to Lorca and saw Peter at the bus station. He said he felt really sick and thus was taking the bus to Estella. The Americans were also taking the bus.

A note about the bus rides: at this point, Les felt that I was not capable of walking the entire route every day and that's why he kept suggesting to take the bus for a portion of it. I guess a part of me agreed with him so I kept saying yes. I thought that he kept suggesting it because his knees were hurting. We did this for a few more days until I thought, this is not right. It was sweet of him to try to protect me from getting too tired but we were there to walk! Besides, we were getting stronger and more capable each day. The thing is, the Camino is not a contest of strength. You do what you can, and no one should judge another person who takes the bus or a taxi. All told, we walked around 90-95% of the Camino and I was ok with that.

At the bus stop, we met a young Italian guy named Fabio, who works in a restaurant in Lake Como. George Clooney and his wife Amal have eaten there - he was more impressed by her than by him. The American ladies Tina and Candy and I took pictures with him because he was so good-natured. And handsome.

Today we entered the wine-growing region of Spain so we started to walk among beautiful vineyards. It reminded me of Napa and I felt sad because it was during this time that the fires in Napa and Santa Rosa were raging. I said a prayer for Napa every day. We walked for a bit with the Americans, and had lunch with them at a park bench under the shade of a tree in the town of Villatuerta. This is when we learned from Tina that the brine the olives are soaked in makes a good electrolyte drink. After eating the packaged olives, she drinks the brine. I love olives and I love briny stuff, so I followed her advice the rest of the Camino. At lunch was also when I realized that there are no garbage cans on the streets because there were gigantic recycle bins and the garbage bin was big too. We rested for a long time because it was very hot.

We visited a 14th century church called Iglesia de la Asuncion. When they cleaned out the church walls within the last century, they discovered 8th century frescoes, which are so primitive and unbelievably old. The theory is that they were painted over during the plague.

Estella was quite a big town; there were plenty of churches and historic buildings that we could have visited, but didn't, because we were too tired.

We had another meal in the downtown area before looking for the bed and breakfast that we were staying in. We had paella, torta de patata and mixed olives washed down with Cokes.

It was here that we first saw chocolate-covered donuts called "Filipinos." They were called this because they were small and brown, just like Filipinos. Unbelievable how politically incorrect the Spaniards can be. There were three versions: milk, white and dark chocolate. Les said the milk chocolate version was for mestizas (half breeds) like me. And the dark chocolate?

We stayed at B&B Zaldu, which was at the top of a hill past the bull-flighting ring which was very underwhelming because it didn't look well-maintained. I had envisioned a grander structure. They also had a jai alai fronton.

It was a very nice B&B though; we had to go up a few steps to get to the front door and the interior had lots of antique furniture and beautiful woods. We had a private room on the second floor, and the Spanish couple we met in Zubiri were in the same B&B. Our room overlooked the backyard, which had a huge swimming pool, but the water was green so it didn't look like it had been used for a while. Today would have been a good time to use it. The owners were a couple who were both very nice, petite folks. He said that Olano is a very typical Basco Navara last name so he said that Les's ancestors probably came from Navara. At this point of the Camino, we were very deep in Basque country. I did not explain to them that most Filipino last names were changed to Spanish names when we were ruled by them. I honestly doubted that Les had a Basque ancestor from Navarre as he is 100% Filipino.

After checking in, we went back to the downtown area and walked around town, observing the locals. We continued to see multi-generational families hanging out at the plaza mayor (the town's main square, usually in front of the church), where the kids played soccer while the grown-ups visited with each other. For dinner, we had different types of pintxos - piquillo peppers, small fish around olives, egg on bread, bell pepper on bread, two glasses each of the local vino tinto and mixed olives. I really love that mixed olives always came with an order of wine. Delish!

Day 7 Estella to Los Arcos

The Man Who Invented Beer–Yoga

We had breakfast the next morning at the B&B; this time, it was served by the wife. She again said that the name Olano is a Navarre Basque name. She had a big smile when Les asked to take a picture with her. She cooked us eggs, and served us a very typical breakfast of coffee/fresh orange juice (zumo)/tostadas (sponge cake)/bread.

Since Estella is a big town, and because our B&B was at the edge of town, we had a bit of difficulty finding the Camino path out of it. We finally did, following other pilgrims. Unfortunately, we missed the iconic Fuente del Vino or free water-or-wine fountain that's located at the gate of a winery. What a bummer because Les was really looking forward to that!

Today's walk was a lot of fun and very picturesque. The backdrop of our walk were amazing limestone-type cliffs that we could see in the distance. We used them as background for a bunch of pictures. I was afraid we would have to cross those cliffs eventually but we didn't have to (whew!). The walk itself was fun because we met Colette, a Frenchwoman from the French Pyrenees, so she was used to the ups and downs of the terrain. Colette was wonderful to walk with - very animated and she just laughed a lot! She pointed out a castle on top of one of the big hills that we passed. We would have missed it altogether had she not done that.

We walked through trees, vineyards and a mountain and there were quite a few pilgrims walking that day. One of the Spanish pilgrims we walked with was on his cell phone for hours!

We went up a small mountain (Villamayor de Monjardin) and there was a cute little town at the top but we were surprised to see that there were also big houses made of stone. One impressive house even had a sweet little Benz in the driveway. There was also a huge church in town.

We had lunch on the picnic tables near the entrance of the church - bread, olives, Laughing Cow cheese and cold cuts and bought Cokes at a little store just across from it. When we were getting ready to leave, Joel showed up and we shared our food with him because we still had a lot.

It was a hot day and while the start of the walk was through trees and vineyards, the road became hot and desolate for many kms especially after Monjardin.

We saw Lucy from England resting on the side of the road with her guitar. We said hola and nothing more. She was walking alone at that point. We would eventually hang out with her in Santiago and hear the beautiful songs she composed while she was on her Camino.

After walking in the damned heat for hours, we saw what we first thought was a mirage, but as we got closer, we saw that it was real. A food truck! All pilgrims stopped there as there was nowhere else to buy refreshments. However, his prices reflected the fact that he had a captive market. Two glasses of fresh orange juice cost five euros! Next to his food truck, he had makeshift tents and tables and chairs. Les and I sat there for a while, resting, and getting ready for the last six kms of the day.

Those last six kms was very difficult because of the heat. Oh boy was it ever hard!

We finally got to Los Arcos, a medieval town with a long, long cobblestone main alley. Our hostel, called Pension Ostadar, was at the other end of town and we passed the church, the plaza mayor and a short bridge to get to it. We also passed a park where we saw some ladies doing yoga. When we finally got there, I was so happy! The address took us to one of a row of townhouses and there was a sign on the door that said we had to ring the doorbell in the unit two doors down. That did not make sense to me. Why not just change the address to take you to the right door? When we went into the unit, though, the address did not matter. Nothing in the outside world mattered. It was refreshingly cool inside, with lots of marble (floor, stairs) and the whole space smelled SO GOOD! The lady said she used oil diffusers from Zara (note to self: check those out after the Camino). They were all over her house. Our room was upstairs on the third level and it had a small balcony. We quickly washed our clothes and used the chairs and the railing outside to dry our clothes. We hogged all the chairs on the balcony until we heard the room next door being opened and since they had part of the balcony, we gave up some of the chairs. We did not have our own bathroom but we were sharing it just with the couple in the other room so it was ok. The bathroom smelled so good. It was huge, with a bathtub that I was tempted to use. The floor was also marble. We crossed the bridge to go back to the plaza mayor and explored a little bit. This is where we bought the local version of candy called polvoron and food supplies for the next day from a local store. The polvoron did not taste like the ones we had growing up in Manila but it was good nonetheless.

Before dinner, we walked around town to look for the bus stop because we were planning to take the bus the next morning to Viana. At first the locals pointed us to a hostel, which again did not make sense because we asked where the bus stop was. But in we went anyway but there was no one at the front desk inside. We even went to the third floor, where the hostel was actually located, where there was a big dining area that looked like it was where the hostel guests ate, but still there was no one there to help us. We finally left the hostel and asked two old guys (praying that they would understand my Spanish, which was getting a workout) who pointed out the bus stop to us, which was right in front of the hostel. They took great pains to tell us to make sure that we crossed the street in order to catch the bus heading the way we wanted to go. Got it.

Back at the plaza, we had a pitcher of sangria before dinner then moved a few tables down to another bar and had the pilgrim dinner of vino tinto, mixed salad, white asparagus topped with a little mayo, bacalao with veggies for me and salmon and veggies for Les. And dessert too!

We saw Fabio and Colette hanging out with a large group of pilgrims. She introduced us to a German named Steffen, because she thought he was so cool and he had this idea of beer-yoga, where you drink beer before yoga to limber you up - who needs hot yoga when you can have beer to limber you up? Later in the Camino, we would become friends with Steffen and hang out with him a lot, hear his many wonderful stories and even see his selfie with Pope Francis.

Walking around town some more that beautiful evening, we saw on the next street, behind the jai alai court, the bars where the locals hung out. There was a children's playground where the kids played while the parents, and maybe even grandparents, socialized and had cocktails. There were also some strollers next to the tables. It was so interesting to me how multi-generational families hang out together in Spain.

Day 8 Los Arcos to Logroño

Pintxos Crawl!

We woke up very early this morning to catch the early bus to Viana.

We left the province of Navarra and entered Rioja today. We had breakfast in the town of Viana, a medieval town with impressive gateways, facades and ruins. It was a big town and did not look like it had not changed much since the medieval times. Cesare Borgia, the son of a pope, died trying to save this town from invaders and is interred in the church, which dominates the town square. We were lucky that the church was open so we were able to go inside. The plaza mayor had cafes around it catering to pilgrims and locals alike. The locals ate their breakfast standing at the bar, while the pilgrims sat at the tables.

While having breakfast at one of the cafes, we saw the Canadian priest who we first saw in Roncesvalles. He was walking the Camino with two other men: a basic-looking one and a darker, swarthy-looking man. Then in came Jill from Australia. We pointed out the priest and his friends to her, saying they were also pilgrims. She said, wait, are they the Canadians? She told us that she met a woman who said that one of the men traveling with the priest was the handsomest man she had ever seen in her life. Jill positioned herself so she could take a closer look at the men with the priest and determined that it wasn't the basic one but that it was the darker, swarthy-looking man that the other woman probably referred to. Then she made and face and said with conviction, well, he sure has a different look to him but I would not call him the handsomest man I have ever met in my life. We laughed so hard when she said this. Indeed, beauty is in the eye of the beholder.

The walk to Logroño was beautiful. We passed a few churches, tried looking for a bathroom in one of them (there was none) and ended up doing the cavewoman crouch behind the church. We started walking through vineyards, which again reminded me of the fires that were going on in Napa. We saw Jill for a bit more and she actually had us try the grapes off the vine.

They were so sweet and brought out the inner grape thief in Les, because after that, he would pick grapes wherever he could. Can't blame him because they were delicious! Anyway, Les loved tasting the smattering of grapes that were still on the vine (the harvest season was over). When he gave me one, I understood: they were so sweet, sweeter than table grapes even. You can make late harvest wine with these grapes for sure!

Logroño is a big city and is known for its pintxos. Abby told us that one of the Italian guys told her it was a good place to spend an extra night. However, since it was still early in the walk, we did not do that.

We checked in to our hostel called Winederful, tucked into one of the side alleys. It had a cute little bar in the front, and then behind it was a sitting/dining room for the guests. While waiting to check in, we had a cafe con leche and a piece of cake for a snack at the bar. Our mochilas had been delivered safely and were in a big locked steel cage (actually, we would not have any negative incidents with the courier). The girl who checked us in gave us the key to open it ourselves and then we gave her back the key. Later that day, she asked us for it again, but we said we already gave it back to her. She found them eventually. Whew!

The room we were in was long and narrow, flanked on both sides by bunk beds that had curtains. They reminded me of the sleeping quarters on European trains. Below each bunk bed was a footlocker where we could store our belongings. It was big enough to hold our mochilas. I had the top bunk and Les had the bottom. It was my favorite out of all the places we stayed. Each bunk had its own reading light and when I closed the curtains, it felt very private and spacious. The bathroom was co-ed but had sex-specific showers. You could rent towels too, but we had our own.

While we were putting away our things, we met a Canadian man who just checked in. He was between jobs so he thought he'd do the Camino but he was bored with it and was flying back to Canada the next day. He was our age and when he found out that we were both retired, he jokingly said that he hated us. Retirement was not in his picture yet as he still had teen-age kids.

After checking in, we ate our food in the dining room, and then went in search of a laundromat. We passed narrow cobblestone streets, saw a nice water fountain in the middle of a rotunda and then walked along the wide and very modern main street which had buildings on each side of it as far as the eye could see. It had a lot of shops from the US like Sephora, for example. We found the laundromat after a kilometer or so and it was Les's first time to go into one. Like, ever. As soon as our laundry was loaded, he went to a store across the street because he wanted to look for a daypack. I guess the novelty of being in a laundromat wore off quickly. In fairness, though, he came back to fold our laundry after it was done. We had churros con chocolate at a nearby cafe and they were delicious (we would have better ones later but at the time, we were impressed).

After putting away our laundry, we walked around town again. We saw Jill (again!) and she told us that she ran into Abby and the girls doing a pintxos crawl. So off we went to find them, and we did! They were three sheets to the wind, hanging out with other young pilgrims on Laurel Street, the hotspot for all things pintxos. Fulvia was so happy to see us that she cried as she hugged us. She said she thought she'd never see us again. She's such a sweet girl!

The narrow streets were very crowded and packed with all sorts of people! Maybe because it was Friday, but no, I have a feeling it's like this every night. We saw the Spaniards that we met in Zubiri and they were celebrating hard as it was the last night of their Camino and they were going back to Barcelona the next day. After having wine and some pintxos with the girls, I left Les with them while I went to the grocery store for the next day's food supplies. Then I ventured out on my own, had a foie gras pintxo which was amazing. When I met up with Les again, he said that the girls had moved to another bar, and he did not (or could not?) want to keep up with them any more. There was nothing left to do but go back to the wonderful Winederful.

Loved, loved, loved my upper bunk bed, especially the curtain. When I closed it, I felt like I was in a cocoon. It got really hot that night, though, so I cracked the curtain open a bit to let some air in. Also took off my shirt, which definitely helped and something I couldn't have done had there been no curtain.

Day 9 Logroño to Najera

Who are These Fancy People?

Today we walked from Logroño to Navarette and then took the bus from Navarette to Najera.

Getting out of Logroño was the typical difficult walk out of a city because it took a long time to get to the outskirts. As we were walking out, we met a German girl named Ana. She was very pretty and told us that she was walking over 30 kms a day. In fact, one time, she was walking in the dark and a carful of local folks asked if she wanted a ride because she was walking in a bad part of town. She accepted, and learned her lesson about not walking when it gets dark. She was lucky that the people in the car were not bad guys.

We walked on a beautiful multi-use path lined with trees and since it was a Saturday, there were a lot of weekend bikers, some in groups, and some families.

When we got outside the city, I saw a water refill station and it had a sign that said not to wash fish there. I was surprised by this very specific edict but then I saw a retaining wall and Les said come and look. Well, over the wall was a huge lake and there were a lot of people fishing! Then the sign made sense.

We also walked with three older Spanish men who were doing their weekend stroll. They were throwing stones up the trees to get nuts (almonds? walnuts?) and they were using rocks to open them. One of the men gave me some and said that we should try it.

Further up this path, we saw a hut with an old hermit-looking man named Marcelino Lobato Castillo who called himself the Ermita del Peregrino Pasante. How did we know that? Because he had a big banner that said so. He was stamping credentials and had a table of snacks and tchotchkes for sale. Of course we bought something for a couple of euros and got our pilgrim passports stamped and took pictures with him. The three Spanish men knew the hermit and were teasing him about his lucrative racket.

After that, we started walking through vineyards again and it was foggy and cool - perfect day for a walk! The Rioja grapes were so sweet. We also walked by the side of a highway but there was a wire fence between it and the path. There were hundreds of crosses along the fence made out of branches and twigs. We also saw a gigantic outline of a bull (a la Rafa Nadal's logo) in the distance.

Before we got to Navarette, we walked past the ruins of a pilgrim hospital from many centuries ago which proved that the locals took good care of pilgrims even back then. We also walked past a winery called Don Jacobo (now when I see that brand here in the States, I always buy it). There was a group of tourists doing the wine tour and it reminded me of Napa.

Outside Navarette, there was a big map of the city which we used to figure out how to get to the bus stop to catch the bus out of there later. Then we stopped at a small park with just a couple of benches and ate lunch under the shade of some trees. It was very quiet, and there were just a few old men hanging out. Later that day, Les realized he lost his sunglasses. He thinks that this was where he left them. Oh well, an old man in Navarette is now rocking some cool Oakleys.

Walking to the cathedral, we saw a small car with very fancy people who asked us where the church was and I told them up ahead (in Spanish, no less). When we got to the church (which seemed ordinary and had the typical huge doors), there were a lot more fancy people (the women were wearing fascinators!) milling outside and the locals and the pilgrims were watching what was going on from across the street. It looked like a wedding was about to start. The guests went inside when the bride arrived. The bride's mom fussed over her daughter's veil while her mink stole kept falling off one of her shoulders.

We went inside the church after we were sure that the bride was safely at the altar (we did not want to photo bomb the video). OMG, there was a gigantic GOLD altar inside! There was no way we would have thought, in looking at the outside of the church, that the altar would look this amazing. The whole wedding party was from out of town, all fancy and get this - there was an ORCHESTRA in front of the church, next to the altar and they played one of my favorite pieces, the theme from The Mission, plus a few other beautiful pieces. We sat in the very back, in chairs that looked like something out of Game of Thrones. One of the videographers asked me what we were doing at the church and I told him we were pilgrims doing the Camino. He took a video of us that I'm sure ended up on the cutting room floor. Seriously, if I was the bride, I would not want to have scraggly-looking pilgrims in my wedding video! I thoroughly enjoyed the wedding and we left before the bride came back down the aisle. Again, we did not want to photobomb her wedding video.

We finally made our way to the bus stop and we were so lucky because the next bus was due in 15 minutes. Had we missed it, we would have had to wait a few hours and that would have been no fun.

We met a Spanish pilgrim also waiting for the bus and of course he and Les chatted it up! He told us about his family and his wife from South America.

We got to Najera and crossed an old bridge to find our albergue. There were small cobblestone streets with cafes and bars. The old part of town was really cute. Once again, we saw the Canadian priest, his friend and the handsomest man in the world at one of the outdoor cafes.

We found the entrance of our albergue, called Calle Mayor, but it was locked. One of the locals told us that the people ran it out of a hotel in the next block so we headed there. The woman at the hotel opened the door of the building for us and the albergue was actually on the European "3rd floor" which meant it's actually the 4th floor (in US terms). Before we got to our bedroom, which was at the end of a long hallway, we passed a dining room that had a drying rack for clothes, then a couple of private rooms, a couple of bathrooms which had big rectangular bathtubs where you also took a shower.

The room had three single beds on the left side, two single beds on the right (which we took), a cabinet used as a room divider and another single bed beyond that. We met the American college kid who had the bed on the other side of the cabinet. He said he played basketball at the college he goes to (impressed). When I asked him what college, he muttered community college (not impressed). He was not a pilgrim because he said he was staying there for a week. The thing that turned me off about this kid was that he had zero interest in what we were up to, didn't ask us any questions, which was weird because we had been talking to pilgrims a lot and we always asked each other questions. I wasn't used to one-way conversations.

We went back to the old bridge, which was lined with bars and cafes and saw Patata. He and his friend were panhandling and I gave them all the change I had. He thanked us and said that they were staying at a donativo, which is an albergue that accepts only what you can afford to give.

We saw Tina, Candy and Craig having a drink at an outdoor cafe - the Americans! Yeay! We had a drink with them, and learned that Tina's feet still had blisters, but she was in good spirits. It's always a lot of fun hanging out with them. They told us that the side of town that we were on was the "good" side of town; this, according to the locals. However, Les and I had to get groceries and they were all on the "bad" side of town, so we had to cross the bridge. The first grocery store was closed but we found another one that opened after siesta hours were over. It was pretty big so we were able to get everything we needed. While waiting for siesta hours to be over, we FaceTimed with our kids in the US.

We walked around the "good" side of town. Apparently, this was the original town, with the church and convent and the other side was the newer part of town, with its commercial areas. There was a tour of the convent that I wanted to do but it was already done when we got there. The door of the convent was huge! It was around 20 feet high and I had to take a picture with me in front of the door to show just how big it was. There were beautiful white cliffs behind the convent which formed a very picturesque backdrop for the town.

We had dinner at a small restaurant and Jill and Julie (from Vancouver) came in so we all ate together. We had a lovely time together, ordering from the pilgrim menu. I told Jill that the handsomest man in the world is in town and she laughed at that. Our dessert was flan, of course.

Day 10 Najera to Santo Domingo dela Calzada

Sunday Golf

Today we started at 7:30 AM, while it was still dark and finished 22 kms in seven hours (we're getting stronger!). It was pretty uneventful, passing just two towns, with stretches of long, long roads in between.

We started out with a few other pilgrims and took advantage of their headlamps and the full moon to find our way. The stones we were walking on looked white in the moonlight. It was quite magical, actually. No one was talking and all I could hear was the sound of walking sticks rhythmically scratching the ground.

The road we were on was flanked on both sides by harvested fields as far as the eye could see. Once in a while, we would see some grapevines, which had very few grapes that were very sweet. Other than the two towns we passed, we thought that the road was quite desolate. Little did we know at this point that we would pass even more desolate paths later in the Camino.

We brought enough food for breakfast and lunch, both of which we ate on the road.

A big hill broke the monotony of the day and at the top was a food cart next to a little park. Thank goodness because we were thirsty! There were stone reclining seats in the park and we sat there for a while with two American women who were doing a partial Camino.

The biggest surprise of this tiny town in the middle of nowhere was the fancy golf course and clubhouse just beyond the park. Since it was Sunday, there were a lot of golfers with their families too. We bought Cokes in the clubhouse but had lunch at the tables outside. Inside the clubhouse, I was struck by the difference in the crowd. There were the golfers who were smartly dressed in golf clothes and then there were the pilgrims in dusty boot and shirts. They sat side by side at the bar, watching the Federer-Nadal match (it was the US Open finals) which

Federer won. Les did not go in the clubhouse to watch the match but he was happy to hear that Federer won. No one in the clubhouse was happy as Nadal, a Spaniard, lost.

What wasn't so nice was that I got stung by a wasp while we were having lunch at the golf course. Ouch!!! It got my inner thigh because I inadvertently sat on it.

Walking into Santo Domingo, we chatted with an American, Kerry, from Monterrey Bay. He had started walking from Le Puy in France and he said that while the pilgrim food in Spain was good, it was nothing compared to the pilgrim food he enjoyed in France. The distance between Le Puy and SJPP is around 700 kms, and from SJPP to Santiago, 800 kms. This means that once he got to SJPP, he was already about halfway to Santiago. That was mind-boggling to us!

The town of Santo Domingo had a big cathedral and the remains of the saint are said to be interred there. The church door was classic 7-doors style (refers to the seemingly superimposed doors); the town square was huge and there was a tall tower. All the churches we have seen in the areas we have walked through so far were different from each other but all of them were grand.

This town has a long history of being friendly to pilgrims and we really felt that - everyone was nice, restaurant service was good and so was the food. We walked around town before dinner because there seemed to be much to do and see here.

There's also a parador here, and it was very reasonably-priced (~65 euros, compared to the over hundred or so at paradors in the other locations) but it was fully-booked. A parador is an old castle or monastery that has been converted to a hotel - they are very expensive! We walked past it several times because Peter the Englishman was checked in there. We were hoping to get a glimpse of him so we could check out the lobby of the hotel, which looked grand from the outside. He later told us that while the lobby was indeed grand, his room was very small.

There was a long main street with lots of restaurants. We had a nice dinner there (black paella and a hamburguesa) and this is where wine cost us 90 euro cents per glass. And since it was Rioja wine, it was delicious! The next morning, we had churros con chocolate breakfast at the same place we had dinner.

Our hostel (Pension Miguel) was so cute. It was right off the main street on the second floor with a little balcony overlooking the restaurants. We washed our clothes and hung them on the balcony. The room did not have its own bathroom but there was only one other room being rented that night and there were two bathrooms so it was like having our own bathroom anyway. The hospitalera who checked us in was very friendly and she told us that she was closing the hostel in a few days due to lack of patrons. We were lucky that we were able to stay there before it closed for the season.

Day 11 Santo Domingo dela Calzada to Belorado

An Englishman and a Salvadorena

We left early again. In the dark, on our way out of town, we passed a huge convent. I couldn't help but think of all the women who wanted to be nuns back in the day who could fill up convents as big as these and wondered about the state of the vocation in Spain these days. We heard of convents along the way that had been converted to albergues or offer tours and halfway through our Camino, we would stay in one so I'm guessing the religious industry is not as robust as it once was. Kudos to the nuns, though, who are enterprising enough to keep the convents open by any means necessary. Bravo to you!

Today, we crossed from Rioja to the province of Castilla y Leon. We passed several small towns which had their own, unique water refill stations. I took pictures of many water refill stations along the way, posted them on social media and my friends really got into them. In fact, when I didn't post pictures of these stations, they would ask me if I did not see any that day.

We had a mid-morning break in a small town with the Italian contingent and some Americans as well. In that same town, there was a church that had a stained glass window commemorating pilgrims.

The path after this town went up and down undulating hills, with post-harvest scenery. This was also the day when we saw huge hay stacks which reminded of a scene in the movie The Way.[3]

The church in Belorado was surprisingly big, for a small town of around 2,000. What was interesting to us was the side chapel, which had the carros of the saints used in their Easter procession. It reminded us of the "poons" in Baras, my husband's family's hometown. We also noticed huge bird's nests on the facade of the church. How did those bird's nests get so big? Was it over time or was it because the birds were big? I hope it's the former, and not the latter because those would have been prehistoric-sized birds!

After a shower, we went to the beautiful tree-shaded plaza mayor. It was very serene and peaceful and there were a few locals hanging out on the benches and a bunch of pilgrims decompressing from the day's walk. We ordered tapas and wine at one of the bars and sat outside. A few tables away, there was a handsome Frenchman (Simon, who we would get to know later) and Andrea, his beautiful girlfriend from Switzerland (she later told us that she started her pilgrimage from her front door in Switzerland. Fierce!). We could hear Simon in a lively discussion with the female bartender. We could not figure out exactly what the discussion was about, just that it was about the wine.

We also saw the hostel where the Italians were staying. We thought about having dinner at the dining room there but decided not to because the Italians were cooking their own meal. We saw them earlier at the grocery store buying food to cook for dinner and also a LOT of wine, like ten bottles. They were a very friendly bunch of guys and they had three chefs among them. An American girl was hanging out with them and Les told me that the big Italian guy was her boyfriend. Must have been a short Camino romance because a few days later, we saw him walking with his posse and she was nowhere to be found. She was also the one I was trying to give pointers on how to use her walking sticks based on the tutorials that we watched on YouTube, but she snottily told me that she cross-country skied and that that was the way she used her poles. Ok then! Les told me I needed to stop giving unsolicited advice as not everyone is open to it.

We had a good pilgrim meal at another bar. There was a few euro difference between eating at the patio and their third floor restaurant so of course we opted for the dining room. No windows? No view? No problem! For 10 euros each, we had wine, bread, and the starter for me was a Russian salad and paella for Les and for our main course, it was beef for me and a pork chop for Les (with French fries of course), and for dessert, it was flan for Les and an ice cream bar topped with chocolate syrup for me. I was amused to see an unwrapped ice cream

---

[3] *The Way*. Directed by Emilio Estevez. Spain: Elixir Films, 2010

bar on a dessert plate, but this was typical. In any case, the meal was delicious except for the Russian salad which was actually just a potato salad with peas. I was curious about it so I ordered it. What can I say; not every dish is a winner, but the losers were few and far between.

We stayed at the Hostel Waslala, owned by an Englishman named Peter and his beautiful wife Maria, who was from El Salvador. I asked them how they ended up running a hostel in a small town in Spain and they said that after Peter retired, they scouted towns in the Spanish countryside and liked Belorado the most. Since Maria spoke Spanish, they could communicate with the locals and Peter could communicate with the English-speaking pilgrims. I wanted to ask how they met but didn't because it was too personal, but I was really curious.

Their three-story hostel is an old building, and our room was on the second level (US definition). Our room was not too big, but it had a small room off to its side that had a desk, and a couple of old bathrobes were hanging from hooks. The bathroom was in one corner of the kitchen, a tiny square space but there were several shampoos to choose from and soap (these were not usually provided so I got excited at being able to use real "champu." What Les and I had been using was a combo shampoo/body/laundry soap in one). Maria did our laundry, for an additional fee. They were both really nice and Peter was very sociable. Maria spoke only Spanish but we were able to communicate with her. The next morning, we had a "proper" breakfast that Peter cooked (eggs, bread, yogurt). Also in the albergue was another gentleman and a girl who was walking with her dog. She said she had problems looking for places to stay with her dog and her backpack was very heavy because she had to bring dog food as well. However, she said that she did not have any problem getting the dog to walk, as that's what they do all day anyway. Hmmm, maybe I should take my dog Simon with me next time? Haha!

Day 12 Belorado to Atapuerca

An Old Friend, an Old Man and an Old Farmhouse

Today we took the bus to Villafranca, and we once again saw Peter from the UK at the bus stop. He was not as sick as earlier, but still not at 100%. Maria was also taking the bus and she went with us to the bus stop. There was a moment of panic when I realized I left my walking sticks at the hostel but retrieved them with plenty of time before the bus came.

We then walked from Villafranca to Atapuerca.

Today we met Yoshi from Japan, and his friends. They all started out as solo walkers from different countries but naturally banded as a group and were walking together for the most part. Yoshi walked with us for a little bit. He's such an engaging kid! He's still in uni and has actually done a project with an NGO in the Philippines. In fact, his Facebook profile picture shows him with a carabao in the Philippines. On this day, he picked berries along the way and showed us which ones to pick and how to eat them. He said that the locals showed him how to do it.

Today we walked through forests, which I really liked. We went up a large hill and at the top was the Monumento de los Caidos, which commemorates over 3,000 people who were summarily executed by Franco. They were buried in the area and I felt a very powerful presence when we were there. At the monument, we met four French and Italian pilgrim bikers and we took pictures with them. One was handsomer than the next. Thank you Camino.

Also on today's walk, we passed by "El Oasis del Camino," a makeshift store which sold snacks and had collapsible tables and chairs for pilgrims. We actually heard it before we saw it because their music was blaring and could be heard from a distance. It was such a strange juxtaposition of quiet forest and loud music. We saw Patata the shaman and gave him some change and a tin of food. As always, he was very appreciative. Les and I stopped there for a few minutes but walked further up to have our lunch. We came to a pile of huge logs which we sat on and had lunch.

Atapuerca is where the oldest human remains dating back to about a million years were found. There was a warehouse-type building off the road a couple of kms away which I think marked the spot where the remains were found but we were too tired to go there because it was too far. Haha.

We stayed at El Palomar, which was a converted farmhouse that looked like it was centuries old (it was). The bar and dining area were on the first floor while our room was on the second floor and the bathroom was down the hall. It had a bathtub that you had to get into to take a shower, and my head was almost hitting the ceiling as I showered. I don't know how Les managed because he's much taller than me. The window was a very tiny square at the end of the long frame, and had a little lace curtain.

Most nights, our room would have two twin beds but in this hostel, we had a full-sized bed, which was a treat. It also had a very small tabletop television and we had a choice of three channels. Two of the channels showed football and the third showed an American show reality dubbed in Spanish. It's the one where brides or bridezillas pick out their wedding dresses and the drama that ensues when their families and girlfriends disagree with them. I cringed because I felt like it's not a good representation of American culture. Of all the TV shows, is this really one that we want to export to the world? We watched football.

Jill was also at the hostel and we had we dinner with her. Dinner was so delightful and the food was good. There was only one other table with customers. The dining room was very funky, with an enclosed spiral staircase and an old rustic kitchen with a big open fireplace for cooking in one corner. It looked like it was original to the house but I doubt if it was still in use. To me, it looked like the kitchen of a castle from medieval times.

Day 13/14 Atapuerca to Burgos

Of Chinese Food and Cathedrals

Today was cold (low 50s Fahrenheit) and it was raining all day - a bad way to discover that my windbreaker was not a good raincoat. The inside of my arms were soaking wet by the time we got to Burgos.

We tried hard to watch out for the entrance to the prettier river walk that led to Burgos but missed it because it was not marked and ended up in the dreaded industrial zone going into Burgos which went on for at least 10 kms. We were so tired and wet and hungry but continued to trudge along. At one point, Les said he was so ready for Chinese food and three kms later, the heavens parted and angels sang: we found one! We still had a few kms to get to our hostel but we decided to eat first. We were the only ones in the restaurant at first. We had the menu del dia (the meal of the day) and it was so surprising to us that the Chinese guy could not speak English - just Chinese and Spanish. Why we thought that he would speak English, I don't know. The menu was in Spanish and we had to figure out what they meant but we got most of it though. The fried rice was "con tres delices" of ham, peas, and fried egg. We learned later that this is pretty standard fried rice. Here in the States, it's sometimes called fried rice with Three Delights.

On the way to the hotel (called Urban Burgos) after lunch, we walked past the Museum of Natural History and that's where the man from Atapuerca was. I wanted to go after we checked in, but I wanted to rest too. Since Les did not want to go, we didn't. Joel later told us that he went and it was wonderful and interactive. Another reason to go back to Burgos!

Our hotel, which was on the second floor of a building was modern: no keys, just pin codes to get in and cool black and white photos in the hallway. We never saw anyone else while we were there. The queen-sized bed with a real comforter felt like heaven! The room was modern, with what looked liked a closet, but was actually the bathroom. It was yet another tiny square of a shower, and what was hilarious was that the light was on a timer and turned off if there was no movement for 30 seconds. It keep turning off when we we stayed too long in the bathroom without moving. Haha! It was also a rare treat that we were going to stay in the same place for two nights. We were ready for a break, and Burgos was a good place to take it.

There was a pharmacy at the corner and we bought meds for my wasp sting mark, which had gotten considerably large (softball-sized and dark red). I wasn't too concerned about it because it did not hurt, but man, the mark kept getting bigger!

Also on our street was a laundromat, which we used. Further down was the cathedral and beyond that, a lot of shopping. Burgos is a big city and we were glad that our hostel was in a good location.

The next day was a rest and relaxation day for us. We went to the Burgos Cathedral, which was amazing and huge! It had many side chapels and saints and the choir loft was grand with its intricately carved chairs. There was also a museum behind the cathedral that had chalices and crosses used over the centuries. The church is ramping up for 2021, its 800th anniversary - yes, 800!

Les talked to a couple of American pilgrims who were ending their Camino in Burgos. Apparently, he met them earlier in the Camino and I just never knew it. He's such a social creature, talking to anyone and everyone and since he typically walked way ahead of me, I couldn't even keep track of who he had conversations with.

It was freezing cold in Burgos (9 Celsius or 46 Fahrenheit). We walked around the shopping area and bought a puffy jacket for Les but I used it extensively during our Camino as a rain jacket because my own rain jacket was useless in the rain. We also had dinner at another Chinese restaurant (yeay), which was close to our hotel.

The next morning, we had breakfast at the cafe next door. It had a big bar, and we had coffee and croissants.

Day 15 Burgos to Hornillos del Camino

New Friends

Leaving Burgos took an interminable amount of time. We started very early, while it was still dark. We started at the Camino markers at the Cathedral, then the markers sent us winding up and down back alleys where we saw bakery workers working in full swing, loading loaves of bread into vans. After this, we passed the University of Burgos. Finally, after several kms, we were back on the trails. Leaving big cities and towns to get back on the Camino trail would prove to always be difficult and even tricky sometimes.

Today we went up another mountain and officially entered the meseta, which is what the flat top of mountains are called. In fact, we think that the cover of our Brierley guidebook[4] was taken on the meseta. We tried to recreate that cover picture by taking Les's picture on the curve in the road that looked most like it while I held up the guide so it was in the frame. Now we have our own cover photo!

Since the crops were already harvested, the fields were bare, and the wind kicked up a lot, blowing against us especially on our last ten kms. We would be walking on the meseta for the next five days or so.

We had crustless white sliced bread (Les loved these and thought they were the best thing since white sliced bread), olives, chips and

---

[4]John Brierley, A Pilgrim's Guide to the Camino de Santiago Camino Frances St. Jean Pied de Port - Santiago de Compostela (Camino Guides, 2018), book cover.

camembert cheese for lunch, which we ate along the way. And of course we drank the brine that the olives came in.

We also passed a small church where a nun gave us a small medallion on a string for protection on the way. In exchange, we left a couple of euros as our donation.

Hornillos del Camino was a small town with one road and a couple of blocks of buildings, some of which were albergues. We got a private room that did not have a bathroom in an albergue called "Meeting Point" which was an appropriate name because we met a lot of pilgrims there. It was run by a brother and sister. Before dinner, we went to a store across the street to ask the lady working there if it was going to be open for breakfast because our albergue did not provide it and we heard that she did but she said that since there were very few pilgrims coming through, she wasn't going to wake up early (ie, 7 AM) to prepare breakfast. So, we bought a big bocadillo and snacks for the next day's hike.

This was one of the funnest evenings on the Camino. The best part was we met a bunch of new people - Mary (a doctor from Germany; it was only her first day on the Camino), Alex and Steffen (also from Germany and the one who thought of beer-yoga, but we didn't recall it at the time), Ross (UK), Alyssa (US) who was on such a tight budget that she just bought food from the grocery store because she can't afford the pilgrim meals, Simon (Belgium) and Andrea (Switzerland) who we first saw in Belorado. We've continued to keep in touch with each other on social media.

Drinks before dinner was so much fun. A bottle of wine was opened and shared and at one point, Steffe gave Ross a haircut using a buzzer. What trust! It was hilarious. I remember Steffen saying, "Can you imagine the Englishman is trusting the German to buzz his head? This would have been unthinkable 50 years ago." But here we are.

The communal dinner was a lot of fun. For an additional 10 euros, we had a communal pilgrim dinner, which the brother cooked. It was paella cooked on the biggest paellera I had ever seen and it was delicious! We also got a green salad, bread and wine and dessert, of course.

The next morning, the hospitaleros were nowhere to be found. A couple of guys tried to get the old espresso machine to work without any luck. So off we all went, with no coffee or breakfast to fortify any of us.

Day 16 Hornillos del Camino to Castrojeriz

Camaraderie

The toughest part of today was not having a proper breakfast until we were 12 kms into our walk. The sandwich that we shared on the road just wasn't enough.

The terrain itself was easy as it was mostly flat, which is weird because we are at around 825 meters above sea level. We were still walking on the meseta and we would be doing this for several more days.

We passed just one town, and it looked like pilgrim central, with a lot of pilgrims resting and just loading up on food. It was here that I discovered that I had our room key from last night's albergue in my pocket. I tried to call the albergue we stayed in last night without any luck. Steffen told me to just give it to the hospitalero at the next town because they all knew each other and it wouldn't be difficult for the keys to make it back to Hornillos, We stayed for over an hour, resting and eating with Steffen, Ross and Mary. We also talked to an American couple, Joe and Linda, who we kept bumping into. It was funny he could remember my name but not Les's.

A few kms from Castrojeriz, there was a van with an old man selling knickknacks and we bought one. The van was next to the ruins of a monastery and a sign that said Welcome to Castrojeriz. What a cruel joke, because the town was still several kms away. We saw it from afar and there was a castle on top of a hill that slowly got closer and closer. Really, really slowly. This was some kind of torture as we were both very tired.

To make matters worse, our albergue, called Albergue Rosalia, was at the far end of the long and narrow town. It was a 500-year old building with additions made over the years and the result was a maze of rooms. On the outside wall, there was a plaque of the Augustinian cordon which meant that kings of centuries past stayed in this house when they passed through the area. It was multi-level and had an outside area too. We face-timed with our daughter Isabella and granddaughter Mina from an outside patio off of the kitchen. The albergue had a washer and dryer and Les and I did laundry. He and I had the only private room in the entire albergue. It was tiny, with each of the two twin beds against the side walls and there were only 6 inches of space between the two beds.

I told the hospitalero about the keys that I inadvertently took from Meeting Point and he took them from me and promised that he was going to drop them off the next time he was in Hornillos. He also said he knew the owners. Steffen was right and I was so thankful!

Outside the albergue, there was a party going on, and our hospitalero said that it was for all the volunteers and hospitaleros celebrating the end of the season. I thought, ok, but we're still walking. Apparently, the walking season was indeed coming to a close. We were probably the last big group coming through these towns and the hostels and albergues were closing behind us. Sometimes when I called hostels to make reservations for the next day, no one would pick up the phone - a sure sign that they were already closed for the season.

Les and I went to the supermercado (supermarket) but it was closed as it was siesta time. We met an American, Jim, from SoCal, who we would hang out with later. Much, much later, we would learn that he was a recently retired movie person who lived in hoity-toity Malibu (Les and I would be duly impressed), and for a showbiz person, he was ridiculously nice and I just loved listening to him talk. He's the only pilgrim who we have seen again since the Camino. Anyway, we told Jim where the supermercado was but that it would not open until 5. To kill time, Les and I went to the bar across the street and had vino tinto and tapas.

A lot of the group from the night before were also staying at our albergue. Mary made me laugh when she told us that she was with three other people in her room and she could already tell who the snorers were. Joel and Lucy, and Christian, from Belgium, arrived later that day, having walked over 30 kms. Joel was super tired and we shared a bottle of wine with him before dinner, to stop him from cramping, you know.

The sole hospitalero did such an amazing job for being by himself. He said that the night before, there were four of them and only one pilgrim showed up so the three were given the next night off. The night we were there, twenty-seven pilgrims showed up. He did everything, from checking us in to cooking dinner.

The pilgrim meal was a fedeo (noodle) paella. I did not know that it was even a thing. I thought that it was a little salty but ate everything anyway because I was hungry! Dessert was homemade chocolate mousse with chocolate syrup and a biscuit.

Day 17 Castrojeriz to Fromista

Persistence

We had a self-serve breakfast at Rosalia this morning. I noticed that some hospitaleros set up for breakfast the night before and then disappeared at breakfast-time, leaving pilgrims to fend for themselves. It was a good strategy for them because otherwise they would have to wait on us hand and foot but there's also an element of trust, that the last pilgrim leaving would lock the door behind him or her. Ultimately, though, I think that it's just too early for Spaniards to get up. Anyway, on this day, Christian from Belgium made the mistake of saying that he was cooking eggs for himself and asked who else wanted them. Les and I, and a couple of others, raised our hands. Poor guy scratched his head but proceeded to cook eggs for us, for which we very very thankful. What a nice guy!

Left early on this cold morning. Right outside of town, there was a daunting hill that was very steep! It was extremely difficult to climb but the views at the top were so worth it. There was a hazy fog which made the valley floor below look surreal. We were there early enough to watch the sunrise, along with several other pilgrims. It was beautiful!!! Our pictures from today were some of the best we took on this journey.

When we got to the top of the hill, we had to rest, along with all the other pilgrims. It was really nice because we met some new people. We met Bernadette (or Berni) from Chile, and we also hung out a little with Alyssa from Connecticut, and the guy from Ireland, whose name I could not remember.

Of course, what goes up must come down, so after a few

hundred yards, the path downwards was steep. It was difficult, but not as long as the upward trek.

The walk after this was long and flat and straight; it reminded me of the I-5 in California. At the end of the very long walk, we (and all the other pilgrims as well) stopped for a snack at outdoor tables and chairs under some trees and ate the food we brought with us. There was a food vendor selling chips, drinks and cafe con leche. Everyone looked tired and most kept to themselves during this break.

Later in the day, lunchtime was a long, long affair at a coffee shop which had a lush garden and statues leading to it. Alex from Germany was seated at the next table and there were also other pilgrims there, all with shoes off, sunning their feet and checking blisters. Mary, the German doctor, was there too and aside from having blisters, she was not feeling well so she asked the bartender to call her a cab, which was coming in an hour. She had a cafe con leche with us (and also checked her blisters - she actually showed them to me too).

Joel came and we shared our food with him (again!). We have him to thank for our lightened backpacks. Haha! I had two cafes con leche, the first of which I paid and the second, I told Les to pay, but he didn't so the bartender got annoyed with me for not paying the second cup. I paid right away, of course.

The rest of the walk was uneventful, with the last six kms being very pleasant. The path was bordered by trees on one side and a canal on the other. This was such a welcome change from the desolate fields that we walked through the last few days.

When we got to Fromista, we found the hostel which looked really nice, all lace and antique furniture, but had the nastiest smell (for some reason, it did not bother Les). We were met by an old lady, who kept telling us that she was the mama when I was trying to pay her. We figured out later that her daughter owned the hostel and she was not responsible for the payments.

Our room was on the second floor and we had, as always, twin beds and a big bathroom en suite. We showered and washed clothes as soon as we got there and hung the wet clothes in the little balcony outside.

Afterwards, we walked around downtown - this is a huge town! - and saw several old churches and restaurants. We saw a big and lively group of kids and their parents arriving in town and getting into their cars. We could only surmise that they went hiking for the day.

We had a pilgrim dinner that evening at one of the restaurants near the hostel. Since we were there too early for dinner, we had a drink and some mixed olives at the bar and then we had dinner in the dining room. This is where I had to send back the fried pork because it was still raw inside. Our friend Joel was right, everything is cooked rare here!

Today was a really long walking day, with 26 kms and 9.5 hours on the road (one and a half of which was lunch). The other significant thing about today was that we entered the province of Palencia.

Day 18 Fromista to Carreon de los Condes

Breakfast Anyone?

We ate breakfast at the hostel before we left, and finally paid for our room when we met the old lady's daughter. It was a typical breakfast: coffee, orange juice, bread, sponge cake. Les said afterwards that the albergues like this charge us too much for breakfast, especially this one since the downtown area nearby served breakfast for a much cheaper price. We resolved to not say yes the next time our hospitaleros ask if we wanted breakfast.

Before we left town, we withdrew some money from the ATM and saw Jill and Julie, also starting the day early.

We're still on the meseta today, and did an easy but a long walk of 24 kms (the guide said 19) passing just three towns. The paths we walked this day were next to trees, which was nice. One of the albergues we passed was renting out teepees, an interesting gimmick.

Right before Villalcazar de Sirga, we saw a bar and went in for lunch. We had just been talking about Mary and hoping that she was ok, and voila, she was at that restaurant! She said she felt better, and that the torta de patata she just had was really good. I had the torta de patata con atun (potato omelette stuffed with tuna salad) which was delicious! Les had the small chorizos which looked like longganisa (Filipino sausage) and he said they tasted very close to it. Of course we also had cafe con leche and a Coke for Les. We were happy because the food was so good and we spent less than nine euros.

We were having such a nice chat when I suddenly realized that the famous cathedral in town was going to close soon. I left Les with Mary while I rushed to town to see it. The cathedral in Villalcazar de Sirga was huge! It's a magnificent 13th century Templar church called Santa Maria la Virgen Blanca. The Templar Knights were in charge of protecting the medieval pilgrims from bandits and keeping the peace on the Camino so they were very important. The church had tombs of Templar royalty, beautiful sculptures and a very elaborate entrance[5]. I paid just a couple of euros to enter and it was more than worth it.

Outside the church was the plaza mayor and there was a statue of a medieval pilgrim seated at a table. I sat next to it for a picture taken by the American couple (Joe and Linda) who could remember my name and not Les's. I wish that I had asked for their contact information. It would have been nice to keep in touch with them. But alas, I didn't. There were so many other pilgrims we met with whom I wished we had been more forward and asked for their contact information.

When I met up with Les, he told me that he met a couple of Filipinos - what?! - named Dale and Eileen at the restaurant. They were still at the restaurant having lunch and we went back there so I could meet them. They were both nurses who live in Dallas, walking their second Camino, and they had also done Camino Portugues already. We walked with them to Carrion and made plans to meet at the plaza mayor for dinner.

Carrion de los Condes is a big municipality and had at least four churches on the main street (and even a theater called Teatro Sarabia). The main street went up a hill to our albergue for the night, a convent at the very top. The name of the convent was long - Casa de Espiritualidades de Belen. It was a big building, four stories high and even had an elevator. We checked in, showered, washed our clothes and hung our clothes outside in the veranda, and then went back into town in search of dinner and drinks.

Since there were many churches, it was difficult to figure out which one was the plaza mayor. We did see Steffen's big group having wine and appetizers at one of the outdoor tables. I noticed that Jim from SoCal and his traveling companion John (also from SoCal) were in that group, which made me happy, because the friends we made separately were starting to meet each other. It was a loud and fun group and they were all determined to find and eat hamburgers for dinner. We told them that there was a restaurant around the corner which served hamburguesas and they were happy. The wine-assisted kind of happy.

We joined them for a little bit and then Mary and Les left, apparently in search of rubber tips for our walking sticks. I found them at a store where they found the tips and we also bought a beanie adorned with a Camino arrow for me.

Les and I went to the restaurant that had hamburguesas and saw Dale and Eileen walk by while we were deciding what to eat for dinner so it all worked out and we got to have dinner

[5] John Brierley, A Pilgrim's Guide to the Camino de Santiago Camino Frances St. Jean Pied de Port - Santiago de Compostela (Camino Guides, 2018),155.

together. I had the most delicious beef stew with potatoes that I've ever had in my life! While we were eating, our friends who were craving hamburguesas showed up. They were hungry and loud and mostly three sheets to the wind. Maybe two. What a fun night! Steffen, Luz (from Mexico), Ross, Mary, Alex, Jim, John, Jill and Julie. There was a lot of laughing as we occupied several tables. They actually surrounded us and were teasing that we were on a double date.

When we got back to the convent, we were told to turn off the lights in the veranda (we left it on by mistake). The nuns were really in austerity mode. There was no one else on our floor that we were staying in so business was obviously very slow. They asked us if we wanted to have breakfast in the convent for a few more euros and we said yes, mostly because we felt sorry for the nuns who seemed to need all the income they could get. Our resolve about not having breakfast at hostels didn't even last a day.

We're *almost* halfway to Santiago.

Day 19 Carreon de los Condes to Ledigos

Perseverance Rewarded

We had breakfast at the convent in a basement room that had a lot of tables and chairs. We were the only ones there. It was a very simple breakfast and we took the left-overs with us to snack on along the way.

Leaving town while the street lights were still on, we saw Dale and Eileen again, and Dale wanted to start the day with a prayer, so we did. We walked with them until the edge of the town then they took off in their natural (faster) walking speed.

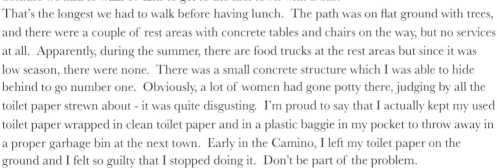

It's a good thing that we had some food and enough water because we had to walk 17 kms to get to the first town with a bar! That's the longest we had to walk before having lunch. The path was on flat ground with trees, and there were a couple of rest areas with concrete tables and chairs on the way, but no services at all. Apparently, during the summer, there are food trucks at the rest areas but since it was low season, there were none. There was a small concrete structure which I was able to hide behind to go number one. Obviously, a lot of women had gone potty there, judging by all the toilet paper strewn about - it was quite disgusting. I'm proud to say that I actually kept my used toilet paper wrapped in clean toilet paper and in a plastic baggie in my pocket to throw away in a proper garbage bin at the next town. Early in the Camino, I left my toilet paper on the ground and I felt so guilty that I stopped doing it. Don't be part of the problem.

In any case, a lot of peregrinos were at the bar at the first town that we came to. The cool morning had turned into a scorching day so we were all miserably hot and tired and hungry and thirsty! Jim bought something to drink and felt guilty about eating the sandwich he brought with him and we all said it was fine. His friend John asked us to cheer for the Dodgers in the World Series. didn't think I could do that as the Dodgers are the mortal enemies of the SF Giants and being a Bay Area girl, I felt that it would be disloyal to cheer for the Dodgers but I said ok because it was the first time I heard him utter anything. Apparently, John is a big Dodgers fan and even figured out how to follow the game via the internet but of course, the games would be broadcast at 2 AM or some ungodly hour. The World Series actually turned out to be a good one, judging by the stories we read about it, but the Dodgers lost to the Houston Astros. I'm glad the Astros won, because Houston has had many bad hurricanes and floods lately and this was good for the city's morale. But I digress...

We sat around for a long, long time, removing our shoes and eating sandwiches and tortas and drinking multiple beers and cafes con leche. I sat next to Mary and showed her my wasp bite and she told me to have it checked at the next big town. The red mark from the bite had gotten to be as big as a softball. Steffen and Luz were also there, newly-paired, holding hands and beaming. He actually went back for her, as he walks really fast and she was injured so she walked very slowly. Steffen's walking buddy Ross was there too, and we all had the feeling that Steffen was going to "break up" with him in favor of Luz. We were right.

The rest of the day was a hot walk. We got to the town of Ledigos and checked into our hostel. This was probably the cutest out of all the hostels we stayed in and I took a lot of pictures.

Unfortunately, there was nothing to do in this town. It did not even have a mercado so we just did our laundry and had snacks at the bar and made arrangements to eat a pilgrim meal that night at the dining room. The hostel is called "La Morena" after the mom of the guys who run it today. An interesting sight in the bar was the partial floor of thick clear glass through which we could see the foundation of the original house, reminiscent of older churches and museums. I didn't want to sit right over the glass because I was afraid I would break it. Mary stayed at there too, in the albergue portion of the hotel.

Dinner that night was with Mary, a teen-age German boy who was very quiet, Pastor Don (so funny) and Lisa, a very pretty petite, vivacious blond American who was very engaging! She was concerned that she would not be able to walk much further because she was injured (she was right: she had to stop walking a few days after we met her). She was excited to meet up with her son, who was studying in Southern Spain. A few months later, Lisa was back on the Camino to finish it. I'm happy for her because she was so disappointed about having to stop the last time.

The nice thing about our hostel is that we were the only ones staying in the upstairs suite of private rooms. As such, we had all the privacy in the world and had the bathrooms all to ourselves. What a luxury!

Day 20 Ledigos to Sahagun

Halfway to Santiago!

We're now in the province of Leon and more importantly, we're halfway to Santiago!!!

It was hot again today and the undulating road looked endless - no trees and we walked on a gravel road. We saw cave dwellings along the way, with TV antennas and chimney stacks jutting out of the hills above the caves. It was a really strange juxtaposition of ancient and modern - if you can call TV antennas modern!

The old entry to the town of Sahagun was a medieval bridge, and there were two statues of knights in a rest area. There were a couple of pilgrims there, one of whom was taking a nap.

This town is amazing - it was actually quite big and had a lot of medieval streets winding up and down little hills. It was like walking in San Francisco, but on cobblestones. According to our guidebook (and by the way, most of the historical nuggets in this book came from our guidebook), Sahagun traces its roots to Roman times and has seen Arab invasions and it is also where the much-loved Saint Facundo is buried.[6]

Our hotel, called La Bastide du Chemin, was an old, old, old, rustic building with lots of beams and creaky stairs with wide planks. We tried using the stairs once but were scared that we would break it, which was ridiculous because it looked like it was centuries old and no one had broken it to date. It was a good thing that there was an elevator, albeit a very small one. Our room had massive exposed beams in the ceiling, which were a little scary, especially when you are in bed and looking up at them, and there was a bathroom with the usual square pocket shower with the whitest and fluffiest towels I've ever used! It was a complete set too - a big bath towel and two smaller ones - what a luxury. We were on the second floor, overlooking the street,

---

[6] John Brierley, A Pilgrim's Guide to the Camino de Santiago Camino Frances St. Jean Pied de Port - Santiago de Compostela (Camino Guides, 2018),165.

and across were two side-by-side churches. The owner said he was closing the hotel in a couple of days because it was the end of the season and that he spends the off-season in his hometown of Barcelona. He also recommended a restaurant in the plaza mayor for our dinner.

After checking in, we walked around town and were stopped by Steffen and Luz, who were having beers in a German pub. Steffen highly recommended the food and the beer (of course he would; he's German!). He even told us that the beer that he was drinking actually hydrated, as opposed to other beers which dehydrated a person. I had never heard of such a thing but of course we tried it and it was delicious. The snacks that we ordered from the bar were delicious as well.

The most amazing of the many churches in town was the Virgen de la Peregrina church where we took a self-guided tour. When it was renovated from 2006 to 2011, they removed a lot of plaster and revealed exquisite Moorish-influenced workmanship. The artisans also restored the ceiling medallions, found brick-type walls, arches and corbels. Underneath the altar was a naturally-mummified woman who must have been an important person because there were papal stamps in the documents next to her. My favorite was the icon of Our Lady dressed as a peregrina, which indicates that this town was an important stop for pilgrims and that they have been supportive of pilgrims for centuries. The church has been turned into a museum and we got our beautiful personalized compostelas to mark the halfway point of our Camino.

Side-story: when we first got to the church, it was still closed and we had a couple of hours to kill. So, we went to the bar at the bottom of the hill and had Cokes. The lady who ran it looked strung out and was not talking coherently. It was sad to see.

Walking around town, we also saw the gigantic entryway of the Benedictine Abbey, and the entryway is all that remains of it. It was massive and one of the most powerful monasteries of its time but had lost its importance over the years as fewer men wanted to become priests. Because it was made of brick, it was slowly whittled down until all that was left of it was the facade.[7]

We found the plaza mayor and the restaurant that the hostel owner told us about but we found way more than that. We saw Abby, Amanda, Femi, Simon and Andrea with a bunch of guys, drinking in the town square. Abby introduced us to her boyfriend (a Camino romance!) named Rome, who was half Portuguese and half Italian. She looked really happy and we all commented on how trim we all looked, compared to when we first started. Fulvia was not

[7] John Brierley, A Pilgrim's Guide to the Camino de Santiago Camino Frances St. Jean Pied de Port - Santiago de Compostela (Camino Guides, 2018),165

there as she was in the church, getting her halfway certificate and was stuck in a long church service with the nuns.

We had dinner at the award-winning restaurant that our hospitalero recommended where we saw Mary, Lisa and Jane, a retired American doctor, and we joined them for dinner. The food was so delicious! I had a beef stew, which melted in my mouth and was better than the one I had earlier in the Camino. I'm so glad we listened to our hospitalero. Fulvia found us there - it was so good to see her! She sat with us for a while and afterwards, Les and I joined her and her friends at the plaza where we had drinks with them. One thing that struck me was that the wine here was still really inexpensive. In fact, when one of the girls wanted a glass of wine, they just needed loose change to buy it. We had such a great time that night and we were both very happy to see the girls!

Day 21 Sahagun to El Burgo Raneiro

Tranquilo

We woke up while it was still dark and while Les was in the shower, I heard the clip-clip-clip of walking sticks on the street. I looked out and it was Fulvia, Femi and Amanda. Wow, they had an early start! I called out good morning to them and they stopped for a minute to say hi and that they would wait for us in El Burgo Raneiro, our next stopping point.

Not everyday can be exciting. Today was one of those steady-scenery, flat terrain days but at least there were trees next to the trail that we were on. Plus, my left ankle was hurting the first couple of hours and Les laced my boots differently and just like that, the pain was gone. The two Motrins I took probably helped too.

When we got to El Burgo Raneiro, which is a sleepy little town with narrow streets, we saw Fulvia, Femi and Amanda having snacks. We chatted with them for a few minutes but they were moving further on for the day. Femi wasn't, because she wasn't feeling well and she was waiting for a taxi to take her further that day.

What a treat when we got to our digs, a hostel called El Peregrino. The owner, a very motherly type, showed us our room and told us to relax before we checked in. After 10 minutes, I went back downstairs to check in and pay for our room but she said there was no rush and for us to relax some more. At that point, I realized that it was siesta time and I'm guessing that she wanted her siesta too. Hey, I can get behind that! She kept saying "tranquilo" (relax) and "no te preocupes" (don't worry) which are my favorite Spanish phrases.

As is typical of hostels on the Camino, there was a bar/restaurant on the first floor and the rooms for rent were on the second floor. We did not have our own bathroom but that was fine. There were two twin beds and they were very soft and comfortable. Les and I did our laundry using the very small but free washing machine and then used the drying rack in the veranda right outside the laundry area to dry our clothes.

We walked around town for a bit and bought the next day's food supplies at the local supermercado, which was on the same street as our albergue. There we saw a Korean lady grocery-shopping as well. On the walk back to the albergue, we saw a group of old men and women sitting on the bench of the bus stop. These locals were having a good time, laughing and talking to each other. We also passed several albergues and one in particular caught my eye because it had a houseful of Korean pilgrims preparing dinner. I wondered if the Korean family we met in Orisson was there, or the Koreans who were cooking dinner in Puente La Reina. I suddenly craved for Korean food and almost invited ourselves to eat with them.

We had dinner at the restaurant in our hostel with Mary and Jane who were staying at different albergues. It was a fun night with great conversation. Jane told us that she took pictures of the locals we saw earlier at the bus stop (after asking their permission) and she asked if they were going somewhere. They said no; they just hang out there because during the afternoon at a certain time, it was a sunny spot, which they liked. The etiquette on the Camino is to ask the locals' permission first before taking their picture or taking a picture with them. They're not props for our social media pictures. It's a sign of respect; after all, we are guests in their country. My insalata mixta was interesting as it had everything but the kitchen sink. It had a canned pineapple ring, a canned half peach and and one white asparagus on top of the greens and tuna. My main dish wasn't very good either. As I said, sometimes we came across losers, but thankfully they were few and far between.

Day 22 El Burgo Raneiro to Mansilla to Leon

A Day with Mary

The walk from El Burgo Raneiro to Mansilla had pretty much the same sights as yesterday. We walked along a path that had a road to its right and trees to its left. The fields had already been harvested so they were brown and since the rains were late this year, they were also dry. The towns were not exactly along the path, but rather around half a kilometer to our left, and connected by roads so the arrowed path did not take us tohrough any of the towns.

We saw Mary and walked with her the last five kms. We had a very interesting conversation, talking about everything from Hitler to the new Germany. It was interesting to hear the perspective of young Germany. Walking with her made the time and the kms fly by.

Mary told us that she was going to take the bus from Mansilla to Leon and we told her that we already had reservations at Mansilla and were going to walk to Leon the next day. She said, "did you guys not read the guide? It recommends taking the bus as the walking path is dangerous because it's next to a busy highway." We checked our guide, and sure enough, that's what it said so Les and I decided to pick up our backpacks at the place where we had our reservations so we could take the bus to Leon.

Walking into Mansilla, we left Mary at the edge of town while Les and I walked to the albergue where we had our reservations at a place called Mansilla de las Mulas Centro to pick up our mochilas. I was a little sad to not be able to stay at this albergue because it was a real albergue for a change. The reviews were good, especially about the communal backyard where the pilgrims got together in the evening. I felt like Les and I were missing out on all the communal albergue activities because we were always staying at private rooms in hostels. There were many reasons for this: we liked having our own bathroom, Les did not want to keep anyone up with his snoring, and it made economical sense to get a private room, which was around USD50 (a bargain by US standards) as opposed to USD25 to 30 for bunk beds. However, the downside was that we hardly participated in group activities. Note for the next Camino: stay in more albergues. In any case, the ladies who were at the counter were a little annoyed that we weren't staying there but did not give us too much grief. At this time of the year, there were few pilgrims so they needed all the business that they could get.

We walked back to meet Mary and she told us that the bus to Leon left five minutes after we left her. The next bus was in three hours so we settled in at the bus stop (which had a bar, of course) where we had shandies (woohoo!) and snacks. It was a hot day and we had a hot walk, so the cold shandies were super refreshing.

The bus ride to Leon took around 30 minutes. As the guide described, the trails were next to the busy highway and we were glad we took the bus. We did see some pilgrims walking on the path and knew that Fulvia and company were among those pilgrims. Les was very happy to get to Leon a day earlier because it meant that he could hang out with his girls. Hahaha!

When we got to Leon, we took a taxi from the bus station to our albergue called the Albergue de San Francisco de Asis. It was a white four-story building, looked very nondescript, actually somewhat ugly from the outside. There was a reception desk and the young man working there was very helpful. He checked us in and also printed the documents that we needed for our cruise which we were taking after the end of our Camino.

Our room was quite large. It had two twin beds and a long built-in desk along the entire wall on one side of the room. We had our own bathroom so it was easy to do laundry and hang our wet clothes outside the window. It was cold, though, so our clothes just got really cold overnight, not dry. It's a good thing that we were there for two nights and there was a radiator-type heater to dry our socks.

We walked around the city, which was big. We knew that the famous cathedral was close by but we decided to save it for the next day which was going to be our first full day of rest since Burgos. We found a Chinese restaurant about a kilometer away and walked to it. The food tasted so delicious! Actually, I don't know if it was really that good or if we were just craving for Asian food. We had fried rice (arroz frito con tres delices - remember the one in Leon?), chow mien, chicken with veggies and spicy pork.

Day 23 LEON

R and R

Today we spent the whole day in Leon. We started the day with breakfast across the street with the usual coffee/croissant/zumo (fresh orange juice) combination. To make the fresh orange juice, the Spaniards have a machine that they throw whole oranges into. The machine cuts the oranges and out comes the freshest orange juice you can ask for. Every cafe, bar and restaurant seemed to have it. Even the ones in the rural areas. (Interestingly enough, I was at Whole Foods earlier today and they had the same machine! It was self-service and you put the orange juice into plastic containers after.)

This day started out very cold, at 5 Celsius (41 degrees Fahrenheit), but I was brave and walked around in my $3 Daiso flip-flops and Les wore shorts and flip-flops. We both wore heavy jackets though.

We went to the first big church we saw, the San Isidro church. It was so grand and old that I thought we were already at the Leon Cathedral and had our credentials stamped there. Nearby was the Casa Botines that Gaudi designed. I thought it was pretty ornate, but after seeing his later creations in Barcelona, it was very sedate compared to those.

We then searched for our main objective, the Leon Cathedral, which was amazing! It's from the 13th century and and has around 19,300 square feet of the most stunning stained glass windows and rosès one could ever see. The windows on one side had warm colors and the other, cool blues. There were so many big side chapels and beautiful Marian statues. My favorite was the one where Our Lady was pregnant and she had a hand on her belly, which was just showing. The self-guided tour said that it was very rare to show the

Madonna with child. Oh it was magnificent!

After touring the church, we took pictures at the huge town square in front of the cathedral and saw Joel, who was leaving Leon. He was a little sick so he wasn't planning to walk a long way. He told us that he stayed at a church-run albergue nearby and at night, the cafes by the main square got so loud that he and his friends moved to a different location. He and Les took pictures at the LEON sign and we hugged and said our goodbyes as we did not know when we would see him again. His little guitar (that was not a guitar, according to him) was still attached to his backpack.

We went to noon Mass at a chapel next to the cathedral. The window behind the chapel looked into the interior of the Cathedral. The Mass was a record-breaking 24 minutes. The homily was around four sentences and there was no offertory and there was no singing at all. I couldn't believe it!

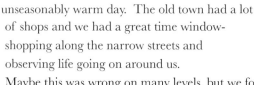

Walking around town after that, we saw pilgrims everywhere! We bumped into Alex, Ross and Bernie, and also Simon and Andrea. We saw an antique flea market with many locals, multi-generational families hanging out in the cafes, enjoying what turned into an

unseasonably warm day. The old town had a lot of shops and we had a great time window-shopping along the narrow streets and observing life going on around us.

Maybe this was wrong on many levels, but we found a Burger King amidst all the Spanish restaurants and had to have burgers and fries. It was a delicious little taste of home so don't judge!

Later that day, we met up with Mary and Fulvia for drinks before going to the same Chinese restaurant from last night and there we met Femi and Amanda for dinner. Abby was supposed to come too but she was not feeling well. We ordered the family meal deal which seemed like a lot of food but we ate it all because it was all delicious, and because we're all hungry pilgrims. It's official: this restaurant is awesome! We met Femi, Amanda and Fulvia on our first night in Orisson and Mary in Hornillos. I think it's safe to say that these four will be our life-long friends and adopted daughters. These ladies were all solo walkers. Their individual intelligence and strength of character impressed us so much, especially considering how young they all were. What a fun night! I hoped we would see them again later in the Camino.

During dinner, we FaceTimed with our daughter Asia, whose birthday was the following day. Our whole table sang happy birthday, to her eye-rolling embarrassment.

When we got back to the albergue, I asked the young man at the reception area if we could have our mochilas picked up from the albergue not the next day but the day after that as we were going to Oviedo the next day. He said it was no problem at all and arranged to have them kept in the a locked area off of the lobby where they kept the bikes. He was wonderful and even said that I looked younger than Les. Wow, what a compliment, since I'm actually older than him!

Day 24 Oviedo

Family

Today, we took the early train to Oviedo, the capital of Asturias, to visit Father Antonio, who's my dad's first cousin. The train ride was long and shaky because it was a local train and it took three hours to get there. The seats were not the plushest either. There was a thirty-minute wait at one point when they had to clear the tracks of something. I have no motion sickness but the rough ride was almost too much for me. It's a good thing that Les was asleep the whole time or he would have been so uncomfortable and cranky because he has motion sickness.

The view on the way to Oviedo was fantastic as we were going up the mountains, through tunnels and little towns. There were trees as far as the eye could see although once in a while, we caught a glimpse of a highway. Some parts reminded me of the Swiss alps scenes in a the movies. I know that there's a Camino that goes through here (the del Norte?) but I just can't imagine walking up and down these mountains for days on end.

It's a good thing that Google maps was working because they did not announce the stations. There was a station a couple of miles before Oviedo, which made it confusing and then when we got to Oviedo, the station was so dark that we could not see any signage. Les noticed a lot of people in the next car disembarking and pressed the button to get off the train. It's a good thing we did because we were indeed in Oviedo.

Right away we noticed how cold it was, as we were high up in the mountains. Then how pretty the city was. The sidewalks were evenly paved and clean, and the streets were not as narrow as the medieval towns that we had gotten used to seeing.

We walked less than a kilometer to our hotel (a real hotel!) called Hotel Blue Longoria Plaza and it was nice! The reception area was on the ground floor, the breakfast area was in the mezzanine and our room was on the second floor. Our room had one big bed, topped with a luxurious comforter. The bathroom was very hotel-quality standard as well - bright and spacious, with lots of glass and real shampoo too!

Father/Tito Antonio came to the hotel. He looked very snazzy, wearing all black, and a Basque-style hat too. He thought I was Tito Manolo's daughter and I had to tell him that I was Bolong's. After introductions and hugs, we left the hotel to walk around town. He took us to the cathedral. It was another big, beautiful one, and we went inside for just a little bit because Mass was in progress. He did not let Les take pictures because it was not allowed which was surprising, since all the churches and cathedrals we had been to allowed it. Apparently, in Oviedo, you can buy a DVD about the church and so that's why taking pictures was not allowed - they want to sell those DVDs!

The plaza mayor was big and beautiful and because it was a Sunday and the weather was good (cold, but sunny), there were a lot of families hanging out and the cafes were full. There was even a marching band that played at the plaza while we were there. Tito Antonio said that the original Camino started in front of the church and went past the restaurant where he has his coffee every day. Therefore, in a sense, he walks the Camino every day.

Tito Antonio (or Pequing as he is called because he was the youngest son) had lots of stories about his childhood in the Philippines. He told us about:

• Living in Hacienda Luisita where they had a big house because his father was an overseer there;

• His aunt who was not afraid to use her pistolon against would-be thieves;

• How Tito Ramon and his siblings lived with them after their father passed away at the age of 29 from peritonitis. He mentioned that Tito Ramon did not have an easy childhood. I had heard that Tito Ramon was frequently beaten by his uncle (Tito Antonio's father), who was a mean man. How interesting that two boys who grew up in the same household would be so different from each other- Tito Antonio became a priest while Tito Ramon did not escape the cycle of physical abuse until he got much older, as I also heard stories of how he used to beat up his wife and kids. When I met Tito Ramon in the States, he was already past his days of being abusive. He had a new wife, but he was estranged from his children. He eventually divorced his second wife, and some of his children reconnected with him before he died.

• How Tito Manolo, dying and contrite, wanted to know if he was going to heaven or hell. He told Tito Manolo that he was not going to hell. Instead, he was going to heaven and all they would do to him was cut his penis off (it was common knowledge in our family that the ladies loved Tito Manolo and he loved them right back). To which Tito Manolo replied, aray ko!

He took us to his apartment in the retirement building near the cathedral. He told us that security was tight in the four-story building because some of the retired priests have Alzheimer's These priests were from all over the country and would be disoriented if they got out of the building on their own. There was a nun in the lobby checking IDs and the door to the entrance of the residence was locked. He took us to his apartment on the third floor where the view of the city and the valley beyond was awesome. His apartment had a small guest room, a small kitchenette, a small living room crammed with books and mementos and a couple of easy chairs, and his own room. He gave me a picture of himself, a newly-wed couple and my parents, to give to my mom. It was taken around twenty years ago during one of my parents' vacations in Spain. We had to remove the picture from the frame later on because it was too heavy to carry in our backpacks. The picture, however, made it safely back to the States and my parents' house.

We had a late lunch at the restaurant of the hotel where he had a regular table on the second floor. We ate an Oviedense specialty soup called fabada with pork, morcilla (blood sausages), potatoes, white beans and veggies - it was absolutely delicious. I then had the bacalao, which was ok, but not as good as others I had in Spain (or maybe the fabada was just a tough act to follow). As always, dessert did not disappoint, with flan and a pastry. I paid for lunch and Tito Antonio got mad at me because he said that he was the host and should have paid for it. Afterwards, he mentioned that retired priests have a very small pension, so I guess he was ok with it eventually. He introduced us to sidra, a local alcoholic drink made from fermented apples. The first shot was sour but it got sweeter with subsequent shots (I only had one shot, hence, a sour one). What was interesting is that he poured it about a foot from the glass on the table. He said doing it this way aerated it more. Dad called me around this time and he talked to his cousin for a little bit.

After lunch, we walked around Oviedo some more, with him pointing at the structures we passed by and telling us stories about them.

He told us about a rich man who got angry at the church and built an elaborate house right across from the Bishop's more humble abode.

He said that the reason there was a walkway between the Bishop's house and the church on the second floor was because the Bishop did not want to walk on the ground and get the hem of his habit dirty.

He pointed out the ruins of the original church, as well as the oldest wall in Oviedo which was from the 8th century. I had my old man stand in front of it and took pictures.

Les asked him if the retired priests still say Mass, and he said yes, daily, but the oldest ones concelebrate by sitting off to the side of the altar while Mass is being said. He said that sometimes they fall asleep and he has to kick their feet to wake them up. He was so funny and a great story-teller! It's too bad that my Spanish was so basic or I would have understood more of his stories.

As we walked back to his apartment after lunch, he asked if we wanted to come up for more drinks but it was getting late in the day and we were getting tired. Besides, he was coughing so we wanted him to get some rest too. Les told him we would visit again in five years and he said that he did not think he would last that long so we settled for two years.

Les and I continued to walk around town, having churros con chocolate at one point but we were really looking for a grocery store that was open so we could buy our food supplies for the next day. Unfortunately, this being Sunday, nothing was open.

That evening, I got sick and threw up all that delicious Oviedense lunch that we ate earlier that day. I suspected that the culprit was the morcilla sausages, which did not seem to be cooked all the way through or maybe my stomach was just not used to their rich food. Because we ate a lot, I threw up a lot. In fact, I had never thrown up more than I did that night. It was so gross. But afterwards, I slept well.

Day 25 Oviedo to Leon to Villadangos de Parango

Henry IV

Today we took the early train from Oviedo to Leon. This time, because it was a long-distance train that was going to Madrid, it only took two hours since it did not stop at many stations and the ride was very smooth.

We got to the Leon train station at noon and decided to take the bus part of the way because of our late start. However, the bus took forever to arrive so we ended up taking a taxi to the outskirts of Leon, to a church called La Virgen del Camino.

It was on this day that we met Henry from Holland at a little refreshment store. Les told Henry that he was the fourth Henry that he had met so Henry told Les to call him Henry the Fourth. He turned out to be a really funny and gregarious guy. When we met him, it was only his first day walking. In fact, he told us that he was trying to get away from a Spanish woman who was trying to walk with him. Fast forward a week later, when we next saw Henry at a restaurant on the trail, he told us that he could not linger because he had to catch up with a group of Spanish ladies that he was walking with. Oh how quickly things change on the Camino!

Today's walk was very nondescript. We walked next to highways so it was like walking along EDSA in the Philippines and the most exciting thing we saw was a water tower.

When we got to Villadangos, our hostel, called Hostel Libertad, was the usual bar/restaurant on the ground floor, with the rooms upstairs.

It was a small town with just a short main street. After checking in, Les and I walked around town, and had shandy and snacks at the bar down the street from our hostel (after trying another bar but backing off quickly when the stench of stale cigarette smoke hit in our faces). The bartender was very nice and he gave us a lot of the usual pickles/olives combination with our beer. An elderly Spanish man came by and asked where we were from and when we said we originally came from the Philippines, he said that the Philippines was once a colony of Spain, as if we didn't know. All school children in the Philippines know that. I thought it was interesting that he was the first one in Spain who pointed that out to us.

After our cocktails, we went across the street to the mercado where we bought cold cuts, sidra and bread for dinner in the room later. We could have searched out a restaurant with a pilgrim menu but sometimes we just wanted something simple, and maybe have left-overs for the next day's walk.

Much to our surprise, when I tried to book our courier service for our backpacks online, their website said that they were now done for the season - just like that! There was no warning whatsoever from the previous days. So, starting tomorrow, we'll carry our backpacks again. We felt that by this time, we were strong enough to carry them. Woohoo! That's when we decided that to make our backpacks lighter, we would discard the things that we did not need. We talked to the female bartender and asked if they wanted my old fleece North Face jacket, my (brand new but never used) sleep sack and Les's (brand new but never used) blanket and they said yes, because even if she didn't need it, someone else would. I also gave away a full bag of sanitary napkins which I bought thinking that I could use them as panty liners, but didn't. The female bartender was especially happy to get those!

Day 26 Villadangos de Paramo to San Justo dela Vega

Real Camino Angels

First day that we carried our backpacks again!

We walked five kms before we had breakfast - the usual tostada, cafe con leche and zuma de naranja at a bar/albergue.

The plan was to walk another ten kms, stop for lunch and then walk the rest of the way.

On the next ten kms, we passed several beautiful towns, one of which was a big town called Puente de Orbigo that had a long and well-preserved medieval land bridge and a jousting area next to it. Jousting! How much more medieval can you get! Here's where we met Australian brothers Nick and Frederick who were both very nice. We sat with them for a long time on a very long bench in the plaza mayor, resting and pleasantly talking about our Caminos. They too were having their backpacks couriered and we told them that the service we used was done for the season. They thanked us for this information and started thinking of alternatives. While sitting on the bench, I noticed a sign at the post office that said they were open from 1-2 PM that day. I had a couple of things (like our cruise documents and the picture that Father Antonio gave me) that I wanted to send to Santiago but it was only 11 AM, and I couldn't wait a couple of hours for the post office to open.

Each of the towns we passed had cafes and bars, but Les said he read about a new restaurant in a town up ahead called Santibañez de

Valdeiglesia which had good reviews. After that town was our final 10K stretch.

Unfortunately, when we got there, one of the residents told us that the restaurant was closed that day for repairs. For the first time in our Camino, we encountered a local who was not friendly at all. When I asked him where the mercado was, he said there was none, no place to buy food, and we should just leave. Since we were really tired and hungry, we sat at the bus stop contemplating calling for a taxi. I walked back to the edge of the town because I thought I saw an albergue there and I was going to see if they could sell us lunch. Unfortunately, I could not find it again. It was very frustrating because we were very tired and hungry. So it was back to sitting at the bus stop and I took my shoes and socks off to air my aching feet and as a small sign of protest that we were not going to get run out of town that easily. Was that so wrong? In reality, I had no more energy left and wanted to rest while thinking of our next move.

Then a Camino angel (a real one) in the form of a beautiful Brazilian girl named Carolina was sent to us. She asked us what was going on and we told her about the closed restaurant, how the town had no stores and the crusty old man just wanted us to leave but we were so hungry and still had ten kms of walking to do that day. Carolina said she would share her food with us and out of her backpack came little plastic containers of cookies, dates, dark chocolate and apples. We should have trusted that the Camino would provide because it always does! Carolina told us that five kms out of town was a food stand run by a man named Davíd, and after that, it would be another five kms to our target town. We gratefully accepted her food and it gave us the energy to start walking again that day.

Sure enough, five kms later, there was a food stand in the middle of nowhere with fruit, juice, hard-boiled eggs and nuts. The kind man who ran it, Davíd, was very hippie-like, loved helping people and told us to follow our dreams, respect each other and respect nature. His stand said, "La llave de esencia es presencia." Google-translate that! Davíd had a small walled property behind the food stand that had a small cottage, a well for water and a solar unit. His food stand was self-service and donativo (donations only). Les and I had some fruit, a couple of hard-boiled eggs and orange juice. Les was giving Davíd 3 euros for what we ate and he said that it was too much. Are you kidding me? We would have gladly paid twice that amount. Davíd was happy to hear that we were originally from the Philippines. He said that he had a Filipino girlfriend who stayed with him for six months so he had a soft spot in his heart for Filipinos. What an awesome dude!

The food from Davíd's gave us the strength to walk the last five kms to our next hostel. The town that we stayed in, San Justo Dela Vega, was very small. The hostel was called Hostal Juli, and the most remarkable thing about it was the stained glass window at the entrance which depicted a pilgrim. I barely remember what we did after we got to town because we were so tired, having just walked 30 kilometers. There's a picture in my phone from this day showing a ham and cheese bocadillo, a torta de patata, a bottle of shandy and a glass of vino tinto so I know that we ate. I just have no actual memory of it.

Day 27 San Justo dela Vega to Rabanal

Joel Again!

After today, there are only around ten sections remaining in the guidebook, Normally, that would mean ten more days of walking but we didn't want to assume that it would take us ten days to finish the Camino. Even this late in the game, we were taking it one day at a time. We were still very cognizant of the possibility that if we were not careful, our Camino could end for any reason.

We left before dawn on this morning. The moon was still high up in the sky and there was no one else awake in the entire town. It was so cold that we needed to wear our beanies and even had to cover our faces with our balaclavas. We both looked like people who could not be trusted!

The first town that we walked into was Astorga and it was big! It had a real town square, government buildings and a lot of restaurants. If we

hadn't been too tired and too food-deprived yesterday, we could have made it here. It had a beautiful cathedral and even had a Gaudi-designed building that looked like a castle. When I posted a picture of it on social media, my friends said that it looked very tame for a Gaudi creation. Not having seen his buildings in Barcelona yet, I could not understand what they meant. After seeing the Sagada Familia, I understood and agreed with them.

We had breakfast at a quaint cafe (the table legs were made from old sewing machines) and met two young men from England named Myles and Chris and his girlfriend Alina from Poland. They were talking about how hung-over Myles was from drinking a lot the night before. The cafe sold more than just food. It had all kinds of trinkets like Camino jewelry. We were able to buy much-needed knit gloves there.

I was a little disappointed, though, because I had a package (our extra clothes and cruise documents) to mail from Astorga to Santiago for pick-up when we got there but alas, the post office was closed because today's a holiday. The next post office was two days away. I just had to resign myself to the fact that I probably would not be able to mail those, and the closer we got to Santiago, the less important it became to mail them.

Today's walk was amazing. The elevation was increasing as we were slowly walking up more mountains. Pine trees now dotted the landscape and it got considerably colder. We met another Brazilian girl (whose name I now can't recall) and we told her that Brazilians have been so good to us on this Camino. She had actually heard of Fulvia and asked for her contact information, which we gave her. Fulvia later told us that we should have asked for her contact information so she could have also reached out to her, but we didn't.

If you're sensing a pattern, you're right. Les and I were not very aggressive about asking for email addresses, or asking to be connected on social media. It was only later that we would do so, missing the opportunity to connect with many people with whom I would have loved to keep in touch. There were a few we never saw again and there's no way we would be able to connect with them again. This was a lesson to us: next time we will be better prepared. No wonder one of the tips we read about was to bring personal (as opposed to business) cards to give to those who we wanted to keep connected with. If the feeling was mutual, they would know how to reach out to us, via email or social media.

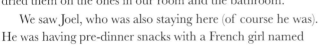

We stayed at a beautiful albergue called Albergue El Pilar. There were a couple of buildings: one was a communal albergue and another building looked like a home which had four private bedrooms, two bathrooms, a living room and a dining room and we were the only occupants. I was so excited that there were radiators so we rushed to wash our socks and dried them on the ones in our room and the bathroom.

We saw Joel, who was also staying here (of course he was). He was having pre-dinner snacks with a French girl named Nicolette, who pretty much spoke only French. They were going to have dinner at a fancy restaurant in town. I was surprised to hear that there was a fancy restaurant in this small and remote town. Afterwards, he told us that they were the first ones there but by the time they left, the place was full. And that it was really good. Unreal!

Les and I, in the meantime, had an early dinner at the albergue and next to us was a table of local Spanish women. We started talking to them about the weather the next day and one of the ladies said that it was going to rain and Les asked her, what time? She winked at him and said, let me find out (as she took out her phone to check). Later that evening, I found out that Les did not see the wink but he was so tickled that the prettiest woman in group winked at him. Oh joy of joys!

Day 28 Rabanal to Molinaseca

Surrender

Les and I had breakfast at the albergue and while we were there, a German couple asked the Spanish woman tending the bar why the church was closed the night before when the schedule showed that there was going to be a pilgrim blessing at 9:30. They asked in English and the Spanish woman could not understand. So I translated for them and the response that I got from the Spanish woman was, "Perhaps the priest was not around. Maybe he left already." When I told the Germans that, they were incredulous and insisted, "but it was on the schedule." And I shrugged my shoulders and said, "this is Spain" and then they understood.

After breakfast, we returned Joels's guidebook that he left at our table last night. Apparently, there's a huge room next to the bar with around 40 bunkbeds but only five or six were occupied and Joel was in one of the lower bunks. We also learned that last night was the last night that the albergue was going to be open. The owner was going to the town where her daughter lived and would stay there during the off season. We were so lucky that we got to stay there.

Before heading off, we saw a couple with a toddler getting ready to leave. The toddler was in a stroller and did not look too happy (apparently, he was crying a lot the night before). The Spanish ladies could not understand how parents could bring a toddler on the Camino. Neither can I.

Today's highlight was one of the highlights of the *entire* Camino. I'm referring to Cruz de Ferro, 1,500 meters above sea level, and very, very difficult to get to. It's here that pilgrims leave a stone from their homes. The stone represents the pilgrim's emotional baggage, worries and fears. Leaving the stone represents letting go of all this and trusting that the Lord will take care of you all the rest of your days. My stone was very small, a pebble, actually, while Les's was bigger (because my problems are smaller?). Some people also leave pictures of their dearly departed ones. It was very cold and the cross was fogged in but we could still see its outline. When we got there, Carolina, our beautiful Brazilian camino angel from a couple of days ago, was there, but she left soon after she took our pictures. The only other people we saw were those who came in a car, took pictures and then left. In any case, being there just by ourselves was a very powerful experience and I was emotional for a few kms after, until we started walking down the mountain and I had to pay full attention to what I was doing. The path on the way down was narrow, curvy, and had a lot of big rocks so we had to be extremely careful. Ten more days!

Although difficult, the walk down the mountain was so magnificent. The scenery was indescribably beautiful as the weather changed what we were seeing. We had it all today: fog, rain, lots of wind and sunshine for about ten seconds. Because we were up so high, the clouds were low enough to meet us, and entertained us with incredible sights. Once in a while, a ray of sunshine cut through gaps in the clouds, lighting up the valley below. With the high winds, though, I kept an eye open for places to take refuge in case the winds really picked up and we were unable to walk any further. Fortunately, it did not come to that. Nonetheless, there were markers and crosses on the side of the trail that reminded us of those who did not make it down this mountain.

On this day's walk, we kept running into Chris and Alina, who were holding hands walking down the mountain. I kept telling Les, see, I told you it was allowed!

We walked past the bar of a man who was the sole resident of that town. We were going to have a snack there but there were four fairly large dogs lounging outside, which was enough for Les and I to retreat and find another place. Joel told us later that he stopped at this place and said that it was an interesting place run by an interesting, but a somewhat strange man.

We had a late lunch at a bar in another small medieval town called El Acebo. Chris and Alina were also there having a very romantic meal and still holding hands! I don't remember

what we ate there but I remember being happy and thankful for the hot food in our bellies. Also, since it was late in the day, very windy and we still had half a mountain to descend, I convinced Les to take a taxi the rest of the way. It was getting a little too dangerous for me, and I did not want to walk the rest of the trail in the dark.

Joel walked in while we were having our lunch and we told him that we were going to take a taxi to town. We invited him along and he politely declined, saying that he felt he could still walk on. When we saw him a couple of days later, he told us that we made the best decision ever. Darkness fell quickly and he walked in the dark for hours by himself, really slowly because of all the rocks on the trail. Sometimes you just have to trust your instincts!

When we got to Molinaseca, the driver took us to a hotel that he knew about called Hostal Meson Villasante. The owners of the hotel also owned a bar across the street and that's where we checked in. They were two brothers and neither of them were really friendly. We were given a room for three people, called a triplet (Joel could have totally hung out with us that night). It was on the second floor of the building that had a very small elevator but it had its own modern bathroom. Oh, heaven! It made up for the brothers' lack of friendliness.

After our daily ritual of showering and washing our clothes, we went across the street to a wet market with many stalls with most of the interior stalls closed. The few open ones sold fresh meat. On the outer perimeter of the market, we saw a grocery store that was open and that's where we bought dinner. Since we were still full from our heavy late lunch, we just bought a jar of pickles and onions, pork rind, dark chocolate and a local wine called Bierzo. The lady told us that this region was known for this wine. Before we left, she uncorked the bottle for us - love that in Spain, grocers will do that!

We ate our healthy dinner in our room. I liked the hostel because it overlooked a street that had stores and apartments so we saw locals walking around, going into stores and going to their apartments. The town itself was quite big, a change of pace from the one-block towns we had stayed in many, many times.

Day 29 Molinaseca to Villafranca del Bierzo

Autumn is Here

Today was a tale of two paths: the first part of our walk was right next to a busy road and cars were whizzing past us. We saw Simon and Andrea at a bar and stopped and had coffee with them. We were teasing Simon, asking if he was sick because he was drinking a Coke - we had never seen him drink something other than wine or beer, no matter the time. Later that day, we passed a winery that offered wine-tasting for pilgrims and we waited for them there so we could point it out to them. They went in while Les and I walked on.

The second part was through beautiful vineyards with stunning fall colors all around us. It rained intermittently in the vineyards but it only added to the day's ambience. This region's microclimate is conducive to wine-making and Bierzo, the vino tinto that we had last night, was its delicious specialty. All trails should go through vineyards. The fall colors were magnificent reds, oranges and browns, and were all around us. Like in the earlier vineyards we went through, the main harvest happened already because there were very few grapes on the vine but what were left were very, very sweet. Les, as always, kept looking for grapes and was happy when he found some.

We had lunch in Cacabelos, a big medieval town that had a town square with several ATMs to choose from. Les was craving Italian food and we found a place that served it. We shared three types of pasta for lunch. They were delicious and provided us with the energy we needed to cover our last seven kms that day.

It started raining lightly but steadily on the last part of our walk but we didn't mind because of how beautiful the scenery was. I even stopped a couple of times to take videos. Along the way, we saw a padlocked blue gate that was not connected to a fence. In fact, there was no fence at all! The blue against the fall colors made it stand out. I later learned that one of my friends, Raj, used this picture on his post-retirement personal card because he liked it so much. I felt very honored by that.

Getting into Villafranca, we looked for the albergue where we made a tentative phone reservation but the lady at the bar with the same name as the albergue said that they were not connected with the albergue and we could not understand the directions she gave us. So I convinced Les to try Albergue Leo, which our guidebook described as a cool place to stay. Besides, the number of pilgrims were thinning out so there should be enough lower bunks for us at this point.

We made our way to Leo, which was an extremely old house with lots of exposed beams and floors made of wide wood planks. It was built by the grandfather of the young woman who ran it. Her mom was born in this house. The first floor had a long bench, the usual stand for walking sticks and a place for hiking boots. On the left side of the room was a glass-enclosed section with several small tables and chairs. It also had a massive fireplace, with a roaring fire because the weather was cold. Beyond that was a bar and a couple of tables and chairs. Beyond that was the laundry area and public water closets (bathrooms).

The stairs were made of massive wood planks. At the top of the stairs, there were also massive doors. Behind the doors was an old-school iron heater that looked like a potbelly stove and the heat it generated permeated the entire hallway. There were four co-ed bedrooms and two bathrooms with showers, one for men and one for women.

Our room was huge, with exposed stone walls and a high ceiling with more wood beams. It had three bunk beds in a row and a single bed next to the stone window. I took one of the lower bunk beds while Les took the single bed by the massive window. The hospitalera told us that there were a couple of American ladies who reserved beds but she did not think they were coming because it was late in the day. Les was so relieved that we had the room all to ourselves.

After our usual routine of washing our clothes and taking a shower, we walked around town, saw a grand cathedral but were too tired to go in. We found a small store and bought a few things for a light dinner. We got the usual cheese, cold cuts, nuts, oranges and olives. In addition, I bought a local yogurt made of goat's milk with blueberry jam at the bottom. It was fresh and hands down the most delicious yogurt I've ever had in my life. We ate our dinner at one of the tables across from the bar in our albergue. The bar was convenient for ordering shandies and vino tinto.

Although small, the bar was lively with young local Spaniards. One of them had a guitar and started to sing. He had a good voice! It was quite delightful to watch the way the Spaniards live - having a nice little drink before dinner with friends before they were off to dinner. As we went off to bed.

We were in bed when, at 8:30, the door was flung open and three pilgrims walked in - Joel, Ross and Bernie. They had just come into town and were walking in the dark for the last couple of hours thereby missing the beautiful vineyard views. They were also very tired and hungry. I was glad that they made it safely to town and that they picked the same albergue as us! Les went with them to find dinner, while I went back to bed. There was no meal so tasty that would get me out of bed. I was that tired. They came back after a couple of hours, happily fed and wined, and they were teasing Joel for ordering fish which he ended up not liking. Apparently, he doesn't like fish, and they were questioning why he even ordered it. Ah the things that you do when you're so tired that you can't think straight any more! I gave Joel my extra ear plugs that night after I told him that Les snored. He thankfully took them.

Day 30 Villafranca del Bierzo to Ruitelan

Ave Maria

Counting down the kms and days! After today, we had about one week of walking left. We were starting to get really excited, but also sad at the same time. And yet the focus remained on what needed to get done on a daily basis because you never know what can happen.

A bunch of us had breakfast at the albergue. We were joined by Luz (who also stayed at Leo), Joel, Ross and Bernie. We had to leave Joel behind as he was trying to book a flight back home and it was taking a while. Knowing Joel's fast walking pace, we knew that he would catch up with us eventually.

Today was one of the most beautiful walking days in the mountains. Looking back at Villafranca, we appreciated how pretty the town was. We walked on a path alongside a river for several kms. The scenery was so lush and green. The road we walked on had a lot of mature chestnut trees on both sides. They were so mature that their branches met at the top of

the road, creating a beautiful canopy. There were many chestnuts on the ground - now I understood why another blogger wrote last week, "It's raining chestnuts in Villafranca." One man parked his car on the side of the road and was scooping them from the ground! The sun never really came out and it rained intermittently again. I think Mother Nature was playing with us. It would rain hard and we'd wear our rain gear and then it would stop so we would take them off. After a couple of times of wearing and then removing them, we decided to just wear them the rest of the way.

Today we walked with Ross, Luz and Berni. Luz and I had a great conversation about family and children. She's such a pleasure to be with and her laughter is so infectious!

After a couple of hours, we stopped for coffee and snacks at a bar in a very small village called Tribadelo. Bernie bought some Tarta de Santiago, made of almedras (almond flour) which she made us all try. She said that it was a regional specialty. Oh my goodness, it was delicious! From that moment on, we made it a point to eat it every day. While we could, you know.

At the same cafe, we met a Canadian family (the two kids were around 10 and 12 years old) and a dog. I asked them if it was their dog and they said no, but he had been walking with them for a couple of days. In those two days, they have not had to look at their guidebook because the dog knew exactly where to go. Another Camino angel, this time in the form of a friendly dog. A couple of hours later, we arrived at another town and Bernie wanted to stop for another snack so she, Luz and Ross stopped while Les and I continued walking.

Along the way, we met a Japanese couple from Tokyo, named Kanemo and Moe. They were very nice and we chatted with them for a little bit.

This night, we stayed at an albergue called Pequeño Potala in a town called Ruitelan that was run by an older gay couple. They were fabulous and actually had a guest book full of compliments to prove it. One of them worked as a chef in Italy for years and that night, he prepared a delicious vegetarian dinner of salad and pasta (with wine and bread, of course), ending with fresh homemade yogurt and the whole time, American jazz music was playing softly in the background. It was a communal dinner and we met Raymundo from Argentina, a young man from Italy and one from Brazil (forgot their names). The Italian guy was teasing the chef about the food, saying that the pasta didn't look authentic. It was all in good fun and the chef did not get annoyed at all. The young man from Italy brought his own meat for dinner, which the chef cooked for him. It was a fun evening, hanging out with people we had just met.

Our room that night was supposed to be a private room, but there wasn't really any in the house; our hospitaleros just put the other three guys in one room that had three bunkbeds and Les and I had the other room that also had three bunkbeds. Our room had a window that overlooked the road. This is when I FaceTimed with my brother Ramon and also my daughter Isabella and her family. I jokingly told Ramon that I had no one to talk to because Boyet was so sick of talking to me. Actually, contacting the "outside world" was a little jarring because it disturbed the rhythm of the Camino. My conversation with Isabella was around my medical insurance, which I left for her to handle and it started out as a mess which I was trying to fix all the way from Spain. In any case, while we were FaceTiming, we heard walking sticks clicking by and it was Joel, Luz and Bernie. We told them to stay at our albergue but they said that they were going to walk to the next town, which was disappointing because there were four other spots in our room. We would not have minded sharing our "private room" with them.

The women's bathroom was newly-remodeled so it was very clean and inviting. There was a lot of hot water too. When I told Les about this, he said that the men's bathroom was old and ugly and since I was the only female in the albergue, he used the women's bathroom. Smart guy.

Raymundo said he usually started walking at 5 AM but the couple told him that wake up time at their albergue was strictly 7 AM. However, they relented and allowed him to actually leave at the more godly hour of 7 AM. Starting at 5AM was just not done! The couple told us that they would wake us up in a very unique, peaceful way.

The next morning, promptly at seven, strains of Schubert's Ave Maria filled the albergue. I loved it and promised myself that after we go back home, I would like to wake up to this tune every day but I have not figured out how to do it. In any case, the albergue's Ave Maria alarm would have been really magical except for the fact that Les had already been awake and had already woken me up. I told him to go back to sleep as we were not allowed to be awake before seven. He said, but I'm already awake and dressed! To which I replied, I don't want to get in trouble so I'm just going to lay here and be quiet until we heard the alarm.

Day 31 Ruitelan to O'Cebreiro to Triacastela

One Last Mountain

The last big mountain to get through on the Camino is O'Cebreiro. At 1,300 meters above sea level, the climb is one of the steepest in the whole pilgrimage. But oh, the views! We were lucky that it did not rain until we got to the top but it was extremely cold. The trail started out innocuously enough but quickly became steep. First we were in a forest and after that, it was mountain paths all the way. The angle was steep and the path narrow and I had to stop and gasp for air every once in a while. It was hard, but not as hard as when we went up the Pyrenees. I guess we've really gotten much stronger! The fog hovered above us as we trekked up the mountain.

Halfway up, we had a snack of cafe con leche and a tarta de Santiago in a tiny cafe called Casa Arbol in a tiny hamlet called La Faba. It was recommended to us by Carolina, who spent the night there. When we saw her, she was getting ready to go up the rest of the way (come to think of it, every time we saw Carolina, she was getting ready to leave). In any case, the cafe was so cute! We appreciated the roaring fire inside the cafe because, as I mentioned earlier, it was cold outside. The funny thing about the cafe was that the wifi password was etched in the wood on the mantle of the fireplace.

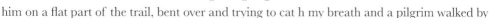

Continuing our climb, we passed horses and a small herd of cows. Les inadvertently left his walking sticks at the cafe and went back for them so he saw the cows coming and going. I waited for him on a flat part of the trail, bent over and trying to cat h my breath and a pilgrim walked by and asked if I was ok. Such is the kindness of pilgrims here on the Camino. If they see you stopped, they will also stop to check if you're ok. In fact, earlier in the Camino, a man kindly offered to carry my backpack for a few kms and I politely declined because I just needed to rest a little bit. I appreciated the offer though.

Today, we also crossed over to Galicia, where pulpo (octopus) abounds and there are good stews to be had. Pulpo a la Gallega is famous worldwide. Galicia is known for its amazing seafood dishes.

When we got to the town of O'Cebreiro, there were no views of where we came from because it was totally fogged in. Sunday Mass was about to start at the Iglesia de Santa Maria Real, which dates back to the 9th century and is the oldest church associated directly with the pilgrim way. There were a lot of people going to church but we did not go as we looked so raggedy, and we were very tired and hungry. And did I mention that it was cold? I honestly thought that it was going to snow - that's how cold it was. I was so miserable. Anyway, there were a lot of albergues in town, which was quite big, and the stores had Celtic-style jewelry and artwork. I read somewhere that this part of the country strongly identifies with Ireland, and it looks like Ireland as well. Even the name of the town sounded Irish!

We had coffee, bread and O'Cebreiro cheese and honey. The cheese was soft and very mild and so was the honey. We heard that people drove for miles to have this. We can see why! We hadn't known about this but the two men at the table next to us ordered it and told us. Thank you gentlemen!

We saw Patata, the Italian shaman that we met in Roncesvalles, the one who massaged Les's knees using a home-made balm. We had not seen him in weeks and thought he was way ahead of us because he walked fast. This time, he said that his feet were too injured for him to continue walking and that he was going back to Italy the next day. His Camino was over. I hope he gets to finish it someday. He was indeed a true pilgrim because he hardly had any money and was able to survive by asking for alms at every town he passed so he could continue. Today my knees started to hurt and I don't even have knee problems! I decided that it would be too much to walk down the mountain from O'Cebreiro to Triacastela, where we were spending the night, so I asked the female bartender to get us a taxi. As it turned out, she was also the taxi driver. I thought I was going to die in that cab. She careened down the mountain with an earpiece in one ear, talking to someone on the phone the entire time. There was a car in front of us that she was tailgating, and it was going fast too. To top it all, it was raining intermittently, which ratcheted up the risk of a crash. Les told me not to worry because she was probably so used to the mountain that she knew every curve. That didn't help. Top of mind was that if we did die in that taxi, then our Camino friends would know that we took a taxi, and did not walk down the mountain. I would have died of embarrassment if I wasn't already dead.

While in the cab, I looked for places to stay in Triacastela ("Three Castles" but none of them survived, just the name). The driver dropped us off at the hotel we picked and boy oh boy, it was the worst one we stayed in during our entire Camino. The hallways and the rooms had a faintly rotten odor, and water was very slowly seeping out from under the tiles in the bathroom. I still feel like retching whenever I think about that place. The room was freezing and when we were trying to take a nap before dinner, I turned on the heater but it was not working. They turned the heat on later that night and made a point of asking if the heaters were working in our room. Seriously? Aren't the heaters supposed to be available when we need them? This was one of the more expensive hostels we stayed at and it was absolutely the worst of the lot.

The very, very bright part of this day was dinner down the street that night. It was at the Albergue Xacobeo (Les said, we should have stayed there and I agree) and it was here that we got our first taste of Pulpo a la Gallega. We got it as the first dinner course. The pulpo was boiled, chopped, doused with olive oil, topped with smoked paprika and rock salt and served with toothpicks for skewering. Oh my goodness. It was cooked perfectly: tender, no fishy smell and perfectly seasoned. The other first plate we got was another Galician specialty - callos. It was a little different from my mom's as it had no chorizo and had less tripe, but had more pork and was soupier but delicious nonetheless. For our second course, I had grilled pork that came with, what else, French fries, while Les had ham, sausage and eggs with steamed rice topped with tomato sauce straight out of a can. I am not a big fan of the sauce part but it's a thing here. They served the pilgrim meal with a bottle of house wine. We had dinner with Ross, Andrea and Simon. We also saw Maggie, the Australian lady we met in Orisson, Jane and Myles. It was nice to see so many people at the bar who we knew. We stayed there for hours just chatting and eating and drinking a lot of wine and having a grand old time!

Day 32 Triacastela to Sarria

Henry IV Revisited

For breakfast, we went back to the place where we had dinner last night. Just like last night, it did not disappoint.

The walk out of Triacastela took us through very high-end suburbs with grand houses and perfectly manicured lawns and gardens on very big lots. It's probably what the houses in Forbes Park in Manila look like if we could see over their high walls.

When we got out of the suburbs, the trail went through the woods and fields. The trees were very mature and the trails had stone walls on both sides. Some of the stone walls were barely three feet high but some were almost six feet high. Some of the walls were covered with verdant ferns. If we ever met a herd of cows walking towards us, we would have had to pin ourselves up against a stone wall. Thank goodness we didn't so we didn't have to do that! On the ground were a lot of nut casings and dried leaves. The beauty of this place explains why this region has such an affinity for Ireland - it looks like Ireland!

I wasn't expecting to cross another mountain today, but we did. It was just a small one, though, so it wasn't too bad. As in previous days, we were rewarded with amazing views and then a lot of fog. We also saw cattle which stared back at us when we looked at them. I can only imagine what's going through their minds.

We stopped at a small bar, which surprisingly had a lot of local men, to have a snack and a cafe con leche. It was at this bar that we saw Henry IV, who chatted with us a little bit and then said he had to get going because he wanted to catch up with the group of Spanish women that he was promised to walk with. Such a difference from when we first met him, when he seemed wary of

Spanish girls. It was too funny!

He also asked for my email address because he was creating a film about his Camino experience. Watching the preview later, oh wow, it had a very definite punk rock vibe, not the calm and serene Camino vibe at all. What a personality this Henry is!

At the end of the day, we were in Sarria and if you walk at least from here to Santiago (110 kms), you get a Compostela (the pilgrim certificate). The number of pilgrims doubled because a lot of pilgrims just walk the last 110 kms. The addition of many groups of mostly Spanish pilgrims made the last few days of walking lively and interesting. We later saw graffiti by the side of the road saying "Jesus did not start walking from Sarria" which was making fun of the pilgrims who did the minimum amount of walking to get the same compostela that we would get. I thought the comment was unfair and judgmental - especially since Jesus was never even there! We don't know the circumstances of those who start their Camino from Sarria and no one should judge them for doing this.

The hotel we stayed at, Casa Matias, had a souvenir shop on the ground floor where we bought a couple of t-shirts and a shell necklace for one euro. There was a 30 euro version of the shell necklace but we felt that the price was not pilgrim-friendly. Of course, now I feel like I should have bought it. Our room was pretty big, with two twin beds with our own bathroom, but the best thing about this hostel is that it smelled so good! It was something I appreciated especially after the horrible experience from the night before. At one point we had to call the owner because the toilet was not working, and he came to fix it right away.

We walked around town - and it's a big one - and had pizza and beer for dinner. I remember that the waiter told us that his favorite pizza was topped with tuna. Gross, I thought, so we ordered a ham and pineapple one. It's too bad that we did not listen to him because when we had pizza with tuna and mozzarella buffala on our cruise a few weeks later, I thought it was one of the most delicious pizzas I ever had. Lesson to us: listen to the locals!

This is the homestretch people! Let's do this!

Day 33 Sarria to Portomarin

Homestretch

It was so hard to not get excited by the prospect of reaching Santiago as it was now only 110 kms away. In the previous weeks, we just kept our heads down and walked and walked and walked. But starting here in Sarria, there was a dramatic increase in the number of pilgrims, mostly walking in groups. Most of them were Spaniards and they walked briskly, non-stop chatter and fun. Excitement was definitely in the air! Also, from Sarria, pilgrims were not allowed to take the bus or taxi anymore, so everyone was on the trails. No more shortcuts!

We started walking very early, way before the sun rose. In the darkness, I noticed four mosaic Camino markers on the sidewalk which were about two feet by three feet big. There were four different pictures: a big shell, a staff with a gourd and a smaller shell, a pilgrim with a staff and gourd and the giant butofumeiro, or incense-burner that's at the Cathedral of Santiago.

It's around six feet high and has to be controlled by at least six people.

In any case, we were walking in the cold, in the dark and in the fog and consequently, we missed a couple of markers heading out of town. Miraculously, there were locals each time who told us we were going the wrong way. I say miraculously because if you've been to Spain, you know that none of the locals are up at 7 AM. The Camino really does provide, you know. The foggy trails made for some beautiful, if not eerie, pictures of us walking like zombies, dramatic pictures of the countryside, and trails that looked like scenes out of fairy tales.

Today's walk was as beautiful as yesterday's. There were stone walls along the trails and the rolling fields were green and lush. Chestnuts and dried leaves lined the trails and we walked under a canopy of mature nut trees. It was gray most of the day and we had to put on our backpacks' rain gear so they would not get wet. The sun made a brief appearance just when we were walking beneath some trees.

Today we passed the hundred-kilometer marker to Santiago. It was very exciting to see. We couldn't believe how far we'd walked!

Les noticed that the churches had gotten considerably smaller. Gone were the big cathedrals from previous weeks. Now we were seeing little chapels, and there was no more need for the trails to go into town and pass in front of the big churches. We learned later that this part of Spain is poor, so the towns could not afford to build grand cathedrals, unlike in the earlier parts of Spain that we passed.

We also noticed that a lot of the towns that we passed were decrepit and didn't have any commerce. In fact, they seemed to be ghost towns, with no inhabitants. Once in a while, we would see cats peeking from windows and that was the only sign of life that we saw.

Nearing our destination, we ran into opposing arrows: one arrow pointing left and the other to the right. Apparently, both paths led to Portomarin but one was more difficult that the other. We chose the part that was less difficult. Duh.

And then we saw The Bridge. It was very high above the river, and it was probably a kilometer long, or at least felt like it. Those who know me know that I have this not so little fear of heights. I just about died crossing it. The walkway on either side of the bridge was enough for one and a half people to walk on. I don't know what would have happened had someone tried to overtake me on this bridge. I would have probably given them space next to the railing because there was no way on earth that I would push myself against the railing to let someone else pass. Thankfully, that was not an issue as no one tried to pass me. Les, who was walking a couple of paces in front of me, kept looking back at me and yelling these commands: "don't look down," "use your walking sticks," etc. I was already scared and he wasn't helping so finally I had to tell him (yell at him really) to stop looking at me. Which he did, so I crossed the rest of the bridge in relative peace.

When we got to the other side, lo and behold, there was a grand 42-step stone staircase, not exactly the best reward for us. But Google maps said we needed to climb those steps, so we did.

Beyond the steps was the beautiful town of Portomarin. It didn't seem too big but there was life everywhere. There were a lot of locals and there was a big church with a proper plaza mayor with plenty of restaurants and shops. There was even a sign that spelled out Portomarin and the letters were around five feet high. A good place for a photo-op.

We were told previously by a Spanish couple that there was a place in the plaza mayor that was known for its pulpo. We never got the names of the

couple but Les referred to him as Subas, as he looked like Subas Herrero, a mestizo Filipino actor. He spoke very good English. His wife, who was stunning, was more comfortable chatting in Spanish so that's how we conversed. Subas told us to make sure to look for this pulperia in Portomarin. It was near the statue by the church, and the statue was pointing in the opposite direction of this pulperia. Love the directions! And it was exactly how we found it later in the evening.

We saw Simon and Andrea outside one of the bars and she said that the municipal albergue where they were staying was not very nice. We told them that we would check into our hostel and then meet them for dinner later.

Our hostel, Pension Portomiño, was up the street, a little uphill from the plaza mayor. We had to get our keys from a bar that was in a building next to the hostel. Next to the bar was a grocery store where we bought the next day's provisions.

The hostel was a two-story building and we were on the second floor. It looked to us that there was just one other room occupied. Because it was extremely cold outside, we were happy for the good heating system because it was nice and toasty in that room.

Before dinner, we walked around this charming town for a little bit and then I told Les we needed to find the pulperia where the locals go. We asked some locals and were sent to a restaurant away from the plaza mayor and it had pulpo which was delicious! Of course we also had a bottle of white wine to go with it. The bottle of vino blanco (this region is known for it) was not labeled which told us that it was locally sourced. While we were there, a Korean couple walked in and asked if the place was open for dinner. The man running the restaurant could not understand them so I ended up being the interpreter again. The place was not open for dinner yet, but was open for drinks and pre-dinner. We ended up chatting with this couple; at least the lady, who spoke very good English, but her husband hardly spoke it . She was very charming and told us about her business trips to the US. Of course we did not ask for their names - duh! We needed to get better at this!

After dinner, we headed back to plaza mayor and using Subas's directions, found the pulperia that he and his wife recommended. It was a very happening place and a bunch of our friends were there: Simon, Andrea, Myles, Joel, Chris and Alina. Here's where we met Jonas from Germany. Jonas is young and funny. We saw him earlier on this day walking in Crocs and socks. And he was holding hands with a beautiful Spanish girl.

Since we were at another pulperia, we ordered more pulpo and they were good but not as good as the first place we went to. Everyone was having a great time! Andrea told me that there was a Mass going on across the street in the big church so I ran to catch it. It was close to the end, unfortunately. After Mass, I saw Subas and his wife. They told me that the priest was going to stamp our credentials after Mass so I stayed and went to the side of the altar which turned out to be where the line started so I was actually the first to get our credentials stamped. After Mass, I re-joined the gang at the pulperia. This was such a fun evening. We went back to our hostel up the hill swaying a little bit and trying to convince ourselves that we needed the alcohol for warmth. I really liked this town.

Day 34 Portomarin to Palas de Rei

Patience

We had breakfast at the pulperia from the night before and all the usual suspects were there again. The other pilgrims told me that in order to leave town, we had to walk across The Bridge again. I was getting paler by the minute when one of them cracked and said that Les made them say it. He got me really good on that one!

Leaving town, we did have to cross another bridge but it was much smaller than the one from the day before and did not instill any fear in me. Shortly after that, Myles and Joel overtook us. We could hear them from a mile away as they were singing very loudly. While we were walking with them, I remember that we were talking about the trees, and a contest between man versus tree to see which was the stronger. I don't remember the actual conversation but it was so ridiculous that they had us laughing so hard. Those two would make good comedy routine partners.

We were supposed to stop walking after 19 kms but Les really wanted to press on so we ended up doing 26 kms today. Consequently, we didn't have too many pictures because today's mantra was keep your head down and walk!

We had a lot of fun during our extended lunch today at a bar and the pulpo crowd was there again: Joel, Myles, Chris, Alina, Henry IV and even the Japanese couple Kanemo and Moe. Everyone was in high spirits. Henry was telling us about the video that he was making and Les teased him about needing his manager's ok to appear in it. Henry then said that he wanted me to be in it, not him. Ha!

For part of the walk, we passed by burned trees in the forest, a reminder of the forest fire that raged through Spain and Portugal barely a month ago. It was sad to see swathes of burned trees. The story I heard is that a mentally unstable man drove up and down Spain and Portugal that day and started 45(!) fires. Later in the trip, when we were on the bus to Lisbon, we saw more evidence of the fires that this man started. There was more devastation in Portugal than in Spain. It was so sad to see.

There was sunshine for a bit but most of the day was overcast and it rained on and off. We actually wore our rain gear most of the day because we got tired of putting them on and taking them off. Today's trails were beautiful, so green, and there were elevation shifts as we went from lower fields to higher hills. The views from the hills were dramatic because we could see more mountains but the giant rainclouds between us and the mountains cast huge shadows in the valleys below us.

As in previous days, we passed small ghost towns where we did not see any locals. Once in a while, we would again see some cats peeking at us through the windows, but not much more than that.

An interesting sight was an albergue with giant ant statues in its yard. I bet you every pilgrim who has walked through this place has taken a picture of these ants!

Palas de Rei is a big town with a few banks and lots of albergue choices. We stayed at a hostel called O Castelo, which was on the third floor of a building. There was a room in the back of the hostel where pilgrims could have dinner. Because we were on the third floor, it had a good view of nature. There was also a little outdoor area, but it was too cold to do anything al fresco. We had our own room but the bathrooms were shared. The bathroom was interesting because there was a space heater that the owners stuck in a bidet. It looked like a safety hazard to me, combining water and electricity. I assumed that no one would dare use the bidet! What was exciting to us was that our room had a radiator heater next to my bed (we had twin beds) which meant that we could drape our wool socks over it and they would be dry the next day. I tell you, the things that make us happy these days are the simple things like dry and toasty wool socks in the morning!

We had dinner at the bar next door. We're almost always happy about the food and service in this area, but this was a big disappointment. We had torta de patata and Les also ordered French fries so we had an overload of potatoes. The food came out staggered too. We were already full by the time the last dish came out.

Today was a lesson in patience. Joel had previously told us that every person you meet on the Camino was sent by God and you were supposed to learn something from him or her. Today, there was a woman at breakfast who sat directly in front of Joel while I was talking to him, effectively ending our conversation. She sat right in my line of sight and I thought, hmm, rude, but no big deal. I remembered her from the day before when she was in a bar with another woman who was translating for her. Today, she was walking by herself and I found myself walking next to her. She told me that she and her family used to live in the SF Bay Area but it became too expensive for them so they moved to Portland. We talked about family and then I realized that she was doing most of the talking, and was not asking anything about my family. And then, she started telling me about the Camino and how the next day's path was the most difficult because there was a big mountain to cross. I was perplexed because we had already passed the big mountains of the Pyrenees and O'Cebreiro but she insisted that her guide indicated a big mountain the next day. To prove it, she showed me her guide and I saw that it was only for the last 110 kms (Sarria to Santiago). Then I understood where she was coming from as she did not pass through either of the mountains that Les and I had to climb. Les, who could hear part of our conversation, started to walk well ahead of us. I knew that he wanted nothing to do with this kind of a know-it-all person. That part really didn't bother me (trying to be Zen-like because, you know, we were on a pilgrimage) but what finally annoyed me was that it started to rain and she asked me to fish out her rain jacket out of the top pocket of her backpack. This was so she wouldn't have to remove her backpack. It was hard to find the small folded up jacket and she said it was difficult to find because there were other things on top of it and for me to just keep looking. All this time, she was quite oblivious that I was getting soaked in the rain. I finally got her rain jacket and she had to remove her backpack anyway to put it on. In the meantime, I had to remove my own backpack and put my jacket on as well, half-soaked by the rain. Removing and putting on a backpack does not sound like a big deal but it was because pilgrims' backpacks are big and heavy. It's a major production to get them on and off. In any case, she continued walking with me, and stream of consciousness talking the whole time until thankfully, several minutes later, there was a clearing next to the forest and around 20 pilgrims were congregated there. There was a man who was giving away some goodies and the lady was interested in what was going on. Les and I took that opportunity to continue walking without her. We never saw her on the trail again, nor in Santiago. In thinking about this encounter, all I could conclude was that God sent her to me that day to test my patience. I think I passed the test because at no point did I overtly show any annoyance. I would probably have gained more points if I didn't allow myself to get annoyed in the first place. Oh well, we all need to work on something, don't we?

Day 35 Palas de Rei to Arzua

Endurance

Last night's albergue was at the edge of town and we were too tired to explore the rest of the town. That was unfortunate because the next morning, we saw that just around the corner was a nice church and the lively plaza mayor with several restaurants. In fact, that morning, we ran into Ross, who was looking for an ATM.

This was a very long day and the longest distance that we walked: 31 kms, but the trails were beautiful. We walked through tree-lined trails, over stone bridges and forests where some of the trees were covered by ivy and there were dried leaves and nuts for ground cover. The path was pleasantly rising and falling. It was not a flat walk at all.

Today's highlight was definitely the pulpo at Pulperia Ezequiel in the town of Melide, which is very famous among locals and non-locals alike. As we came out of the forest and into town, the first pulperia that we passed was giving away samples of pulpo, enticing the pilgrims to eat there. It was delicious and we almost ate there but a young (and extremely handsome) Spanish pilgrim named Jorge tapped Les's arm and said go to Ezequiel, it's the best one. So we walked a few hundred feet more to get there. And thank goodness that we did!

As we walked into this pulperia, we saw a counter to our right and behind it, giant pots of boiled octopus. The man at the counter asked us if we also needed a room at their albergue, which we did not as we planned to walk more that day. Because we were very hungry, we asked for two orders of pulpo and a bottle of vino blanco that this area was known for and happened to go very well with pulpo.

The communal tables were long slabs of wood. We sat at the end of one in the front dining area that had an elaborate mural along its wall depicting the Camino's stages. The rest rooms, which I used, were in the rear of the restaurant and to get there, I passed a huge interior dining area which had many more tables. The staff was setting up lunch for a tour group of about a

hundred people who were coming by bus. They had all the place settings ready, and were putting a salad on top of each of the plates. On a sideboard, there were cakes cut into pieces, presumably for dessert. The depth and the size of the restaurant was impressive and a surprise because the entrance was not that wide.

Our pulpo and wine arrived with bread and wow, this place was worth going the extra hundred steps for. It did not disappoint at all! The pulpo was served on a wood plate with

toothpicks for picking and the wine was served in footed green cups that were white on the inside, which was the tradition in the area. Like the pulpo from the other night, it was simply boiled to perfection and topped with olive oil and seasoned with smoked paprika and rock salt. The wine was very local, its label showing that it was from Melide, and tasted like pinot grigio. Les and I were so hungry that we ate every last bit of our food and wiped our plates clean with the bread.

A few tables away, Chris and Alina were also having lunch. On their way out, they told us that they were headed to a local churreria for dessert and to make sure that we went there too. He said that it was highly recommended in his guidebook. I guess we had no choice but to go!

The churros con chocolate at that little hole in the wall churreria was the most delicious we would have in all of Spain.

The churros were golden strips of pastry and the chocolate was the darkest, thickest chocolate we had. I suspect that if allowed to get cold, it would form a solid block of chocolate. We also enjoyed the company of Chris and Alina while having dessert.

The big problem was that after our extended and heavy lunch, it was around 2 PM and we still had to walk 15 more kms to our destination. We were both full and I was slightly inebriated and not looking forward to the afternoon walk at all.

It was definitely not an easy walk and we were very tired. I was slightly apprehensive because it was the latest in the day that we had to walk. The days had become shorter, with the time change and the season, and I did not want to walk in the dark like some of our young Camino friends did.

Around seven kms before Arzua, we passed through a town where we saw an albergue that had the name of the one we had reservations for but it was confusing because we were not yet at the town we wanted to stop. I talked to the lady who was there and she said they were closed for the season and that up ahead in Arzua was an albergue of the same name. So we continued walking and the path became a little confusing and there were no other pilgrims to follow. We came upon a busy freeway and Google maps indicated that we needed to turn right and walk along it to get to the town while the Camino arrow told us to turn left. Les said that there was no way he was going to walk along the highway.

Les won this argument and we went left. I'm so glad we did because lo and behold, there was an underpass made for pedestrians and pilgrims like us. We ended up on the other side, safe and sound and that's when we turned right. We managed to slog through the last five or so kms to town, which had a very long main road. The town was actually quite big, with a lot of side streets, apartments, albergues and commercial establishments catering to agriculture.

We still had a few hundred feet to walk when we saw the wife of Subas. She told us that she and her husband were staying at the hotel called Pension Teodora across the street. She highly recommended it and said that it's where they always stay when they walk the Camino. She was our Camino Angel that day because we did not have the strength to walk any further. She also told us that the restaurant on the premises served delicious pilgrim dinners. Sold! The hotel turned out to be perfectly located as behind it was the albergue where Joel, Myles and Ross were staying. We finally got savvy enough to text each other (which we should have been doing all along - texting people we've met and arranging to meet for dinner if we were in the same town) and decided to meet at the restaurant in the hotel. The restaurant looked expensive, being in a hotel and the tables had green linen but the pilgrim menu was still 11 euros. It was so funny because from the window by our table, we could see their albergue and the laundry room. This way, Joel, who was doing laundry, could keep track of his laundry.

What a fun dinner! I can't remember exactly what we ate; I just remember that it was delicious all the way to dessert. We had a good conversation about our Camino experiences, people we'd met along the way and how far we'd all come. We only had two more days of walking left! Myles, Joel and Ross had us laughing all night and they got funnier as we drank more wine. Part of the conversation, though, was very deep and serious. We talked about what was unexpected and what we leaned on our Camino experience. At the end of the meal, we ordered brightly-colored shots of yellow alcohol (for an extra euro), which was a local drink that we were curious about. We chugged it and I remember it tasting like a lemony cough syrup.

After we said our goodbyes, to their surprise, Les and I walked towards the elevator. They said what? You guys are staying here? Of course you are! There was a lot of eye-rolling followed by laughter all around. And with that, they proceeded to their albergue while we went upstairs to our beautiful bed in our beautiful room that had a beautiful bathroom. Sometimes, age has its privileges.

Day 36 Arzua to Pedruozo

Last Dinner on the Road

Today's walk was supposed to be sunny but it really wasn't. The scenery was very pleasant and there were many more pilgrims on the trail, most of whom I had never seen. The trail was interesting and we walked through eucalyptus forests with lots of ferns, and we also walked along the road and through neighborhoods and villages. We even had to go down a tunnel to get to the other side of the road.

Les had a chance to chat with Vince from Melbourne, who was walking by himself. Vince was one of the nicest guys we met on the Camino. He's very Catholic and proud of it. Vince was carrying a light pack because all of his luggage got lost in transit so he only had a small backpack with a couple of extra items of clothing. He told us that since he had several connecting flights between Melbourne and Spain, each of the carriers were pointing fingers at the other. I really hope that he gets his luggage at some point in the future.

While walking with Vince, we passed what seemed like an outside restaurant that had hundreds of beer bottles on its stone fence and bunches of them hanging from a tree. It was so strange that most of the pilgrims walking by stopped to take pictures, as we did!

I dedicated today's walk to a pilgrim who died along the way in 1993. He had one more day of walking to do, practically knocking at the door of the cathedral, but did not make it. There was a commemorative plaque outside Salceda at the spot where he died. It goes to show that nothing is guaranteed in life. This is the reason why we never made plans for more than two days in advance. There was really no way of knowing if and when our Camino would end, by injury or illness or whatever other reason. Near the plaque, there was a group of workers cleaning the Camino markers. I was surprised to see that but it made sense because most of the markers were in good shape but there were a few that had a lot of graffiti on them, which was deplorable.

Today's lunch was a nice surprise. We ate at a sports bar in the town of O Empalme, which was full of local employees who were already drinking. It was Friday so I guess people were already letting loose. The ceiling of the bar displayed scarves showing many different football teams and there was a billiard room in the back. It was a pretty lively scene.

The menu had hamburguesas for three euros and hamburguesas con bacon for the same price. Which do you think we ordered? Of course we got two of the hamburguesas con bacon and what we got were the biggest hamburger sandwiches we ever saw. The burgers on a thick roll had a lot of greens and roasted red bell peppers and their idea of bacon was a big slice of pork that covered the entire patty! We had fries with our burgers and the man at the bar gave us packets of catsup because he said that he knew that Americans liked catsup with their fries. We appreciated that!

It never ceased to amaze me that many times, we're walking for a long time in the forest, and then come out of the forest right into a full-blown town. This was our experience today as well. As we walked further into town (this was a pretty big one), we passed by a lively school yard and it was school pick-up time so there were a lot of cars and parents and grandparents picking up children.

Les said that he thought that the albergues were on the right side of town, while it seemed to me, based on Google maps, that we had to turn left to get to the albergues. I told him to go right while I sat down to rest and if he found albergues there, to text me and I would join him.

I waited for around 20 minutes and was texting him but he did not respond. Finally, he showed up and said that there were no albergues on that side of town but he said he was walking in the forest with a bunch of Filipino people. Uhm, can you say that again? He saw a group of Filipino pilgrims who were on a bus tour but who were walking the last couple of days to Santiago. When they saw him, they said hola, and he said, "Hola? Gusto n'yong magpa-hula?" (Hola sounds like hula, which in Pilipino means fortune-telling so Les basically asked if they wanted their fortunes told). They laughed and asked him if he was part of a group tour. Les said no and proceeded to regale them with stories of how far we had walked and they were very impressed. After not seeing Filipinos in two months (aside from the couple from Dallas), Les was happy to be with a bunch of our countrymen. Les hoped that we would see them the next day in Santiago because they were very nice. I can't believe I missed all that! I wanted to see Filipinos too!

We went to the other side of town and went to a hostel called Pension Pedruozo Pino, which was a big building on the main street. We got there just in time as the hospitalera was getting ready to go home. Our room was on the third floor and did not have its own bathroom. That was ok, though, since there was only one other room occupied on our floor. The dearth of pilgrims at this time of the year was the reason why hostels close after the season is over. Most pilgrims now stayed in albergues, which are almost empty as well so everyone was pretty much guaranteed a lower bunk bed, and albergues were cheaper. However, Les still didn't want to stay at albergues because he wanted his own bathroom and he didn't want to bother the other pilgrims with his snoring. Besides, for two people, it's cost effective: just add a few more euros, and we have our own room!

We met up with Ross, Joel and Myles for drinks before dinner and had a great time. Afterwards, we all went out to dinner with Vince as well. At the restaurant, we saw the Korean couple having dinner with a French father and son. The older Frenchman was in his 80s and his son was in his 60s. Les had chatted with them before at our coffee stops. The older man was amazing, big and strong, and had been walking from SJPP. We didn't ask for their names, again, and we should have!

We had the most enjoyable dinner as the conversation was jovial and flowed easily. I sat next to Vince and learned more about him - his family, and what he did in Australia. I also learned that he has worked for the Catholic Church for many years. We really liked Vince.

The food tonight was plentiful and delicious. We ordered soup for our first course, and since most of us ordered it, it came in soup tureens, which the waiter refilled. We must have been really hungry because we finished even the second serving! For our second course, we ordered slices of fried pork and another meat dish (I can't remember what) and they came on two large platters, with the ubiquitous French fries. As hungry as we all were, we could not finish all the food they served us. Bread, dessert and wine came with the meal as customary when ordering the peregrino dinner. I don't remember what dessert I had but it was probably flan, because I was trying to eat as much flan as I could while I was in Spain.

After dinner, a few of us went back to the bar where we had pre-dinner drinks, for more drinks. We all knew that we just had one more day left on this journey so it was almost as if we wanted to squeeze in as much time as we could together. The only reason we had to leave was because the albergue where Joel and Myles were staying had a curfew of 11 PM. Les and I made our way back to our hostel as well.

When we got there, I saw all the keys hanging by the front foyer. There was no one working and we had the building all to ourselves. I remember thinking that we could have asked Joel and Myles to stay at our hostel and pick whichever room they wanted.

Day 37 Pedruozo to Santiago

Success!

This is it! The last day of walking! We woke up bright and early and started off as soon as the sun came up. Pilgrims were already in walking mode and groups were skipping along excitedly. They were even singing songs and shouting to each other in good fun. There were a lot of Spaniards walking in groups and they were very boisterous and happy.

I myself was running on fumes and dragging the whole time. Maybe it was the late nights or just the cumulative fatigue, but of all the days to have a bad day, I couldn't believe that it had to be today.

One of the groups we passed was comprised of young American men. They were taking turns pushing one of their friends, a disabled man who was in a modified wheelchair. We talked to them for a little bit and found out that they started in Sarria and that they knew each other through school. We thought that it was so cool, what they were doing, and made sure their friend was also with them. After we got back from the Camino, Les bought a DVD called "I'll Push You" which was about one friend pushing his best friend in a wheelchair, and the volunteers who helped along the way. I was crying the whole movie.[8]
Anyway, we found out later that the group of Americans had traveled to other places like Machu Picchu.

We also stopped for two Spanish ladies who were sitting by the side of the road, to see if they were ok. They just needed to rest, they said. Les was tickled pink when they asked to take a picture with him. Again, we did not ask their names, which we should have.

We had lunch in a small bar in a town that was around 10 kms from

---

[8] *I'll Push You*, Emota, Inc 2017

the edge of Santiago. Vince and Don (from Atlanta) were there, having bocadillos. It was a good thing that we saw how big the sandwiches were because instead of ordering one each, Les and I just split one. The lady at the bar told us that it was around seven kms to the edge of Santiago and another seven to get to the Cathedral. I did not want to believe her, but she was right.

Before we reached Santiago, we passed through Monte de Gozo, which was a big park on a hill that had a huge modern sculpture. Kanemo and Moe were there and explained to us that traditionally, pilgrims would see the cathedral for the first time from here. There was even a guide on one of the plaques showing where to look. Alas, the spot where the cathedral was supposed to be was covered by a tall tree so we couldn't see it! The first view of Santiago gave me chills though. We were so close!!!

It was a few more kms to the edge of town, and another seven to the cathedral. We briefly made another stop (five minutes) because I was complaining to Les that I was too tired and I felt that he was not listening to me. He just wanted to keep going and get to the Cathedral fully exhausted. I also know that it was hard for him to start walking again after a long period of rest because his knees hurt before they warmed up but today I was not in the mood to be understanding of that.

In short, we walked through the outskirts of the city having an extended heated argument. I'm not proud of it now, but this is what happened. He finally agreed to stop somewhere for a snack and a Coke because he said his legs were cramping. We were both in a very bad mood the whole time.

We finally got to the old part of the city which is where the cathedral was located. You would think that it would be easy to find a big cathedral but because the streets were narrow, we couldn't find it. We were walking in circles, getting even more annoyed with each other, and just as I was about to explode, we heard voices calling to us - Les! Kitos! It was Ross, Myles and

Joel, our three amigos. In fact, they had just been telling each other "I bet you we'll see Les and Kitos soon" when they saw us. Our three amigos were our Camino angels on our final day of walking because seeing them made Les and I stop fighting. In fact, I whispered to Les, you are so lucky they showed up when they did. Last day of the Camino and we still needed Camino angels! Nothing is guaranteed. You think you're home free, then crap happens and you are thankful for divine intervention, *until the very last day*. I can never thank these three guys enough because they stopped me from saying things I knew I would have regretted later. At this point, my anger had miraculously dissipated completely.

I reflected on this incident later and thought about some homilies I heard in church. Our priest said that the devil tempts you the most when you are in a state of grace. All the days leading to Santiago brought us into an increasing state of grace and introspection and on the last day was when the disruption and chaotic feelings happened. The devil is real and it almost won today.

We gave the guys big hugs and looked for the cathedral together. We listened for the sound of bagpipes (watch any YouTube video of Santiago and you'll see a man or woman playing bagpipes by the cathedral) and made our way down the tunnel leading to the cathedral, recording our walk, and when we got to the other side, all we could do was stare at the cathedral, give each other more hugs and cry a bit. Les and I were very emotional and gave each other a big hug, and we were both in tears. This was a big accomplishment that would take days or maybe even months to sink in. We greeted the other pilgrims who were arriving and we were so happy that we all made it. We slumped on the ground in front of the cathedral with a few  other pilgrims in the humongous church square for a while. We just stared at it for a long time.

There were a couple of Filipino tour groups in the square and Les and I went over to see if they were the ones he saw the day before in the forest. Unfortunately, they were not. We talked to a couple of them and asked where they came from and they said that they were part of a group tour that had driven up from Fatima the day before and that they were going to Leon the next day. They did not ask us any questions about what we were doing there so we bade them a good day and went back to our little group.

The facade of the cathedral was under repair and the scaffolding stretched up as high as the church spires. It was beautiful, nonetheless. It took us a lot of days and footsteps to get here and we were just so happy to finally see it. Have I already said how happy we were?

Out of nowhere came Abby, our first Camino friend so it was a full circle. She was our alpha and our omega. She and Rome arrived the day before but put off getting their compostelas until today. We were extremely happy to see her and there were plenty of hugs all around. I assumed that we would see her again, as we were all in Santiago but never did.

We then went to the cathedral office to get our compostelas. The line was short, with only around 10 people in front of us. We were all joking that we hoped we would pass the test, which we all did. I got two certificates: the original one and the personalized one with a cardboard cylinder container (for an extra five euros). Les got only the traditional one, thinking at the time that it was all he needed. We went back the next day so he could get the other one, because he found out that we all got both compostelas.

The original compostela has not changed over the centuries of the Camino. It is written in Latin and has the pilgrim's name on it, and the Latin version of the pilgrim's name if it exists. The personalized one has the pilgrim's name, his or her starting point, the start and end dates and the number of kms walked. Ours showed that we started in Saint Jean Pied de Port on October 6, 2017 and finished on November 11, 2017 and that we walked 799 kms. That last bit of information surprised me because there was a huge sign in Roncesvalles (the first town we hit in Spain after crossing the Pyrenees) that said Santiago de Compostela was 790 kms away. We had already walked 25 kms up to that point so my total was 815. Of course I did not argue with the lady at the Cathedral office but I wanted to whisper to her, can you please round it up to 800? Pretty please? But I did not say anything so 799 kms it is!

Afterwards, we sat at an outdoor table at a bar across from the entrance of the cathedral office. Over beers and snacks we loudly cheered the pilgrims who were arriving to get their compostelas. There was a group of Italians at the next table and they were actually singing to them. We were so happy, they were so happy, we were all so happy! None of us wanted this feeling to end, this we made it, we got here feeling. I love that we were able to walk in together with these three guys for whom we now have so much affection.

Later in the day, we checked in to our AirBnb that was in a building at the edge of old Santiago. Like Pamplona, Leon and Burgos, Santiago is a big city and a part of it is the original, medieval city. Here, the streets are cobblestone, windy and narrow. Most of the area now caters to tourists with restaurants, shops selling tchotchkes, tarta de Santiago, anything that had Santiago on it like t-shirts, magnets, tiles and anything else you can think of. I saw a couple of college-age kids wearing hoodies that said USC and I thought, oh, they're from the University of Southern California until we saw the University of Santiago de Compostela in old town. We even went into the lobby of the school and almost bought a sweatshirt.

Our Airbnb was on the third floor of the building at the edge of old Santiago, facing the mall. In this case, "mall" meant park, not a shopping mall, and thank goodness for that! A lot of families were going in to enjoy the park but we were content to just look at it. The apartment had two bedrooms, and a sofa bed in the living room. It had a small kitchen and table and the best part was that it had two bathrooms that were identical and next to each other. Les and I took the back bedroom. The bed was slightly bigger than a twin-sized bed, but we did not want the sofa bed nor the two twin beds. Enough of twin beds! Joel, Myles and Ross stayed with us. We charged the kids the cost of staying in an albergue (eight euros) while Les and I picked up the rest of the tab. We never told them how much the entire apartment cost.

We went out to dinner and saw other pilgrims and had a great time. We were told by other pilgrims who had done the Camino before that we would get sticker shock in Santiago. Sure enough, food cost twice as much here as the pilgrim menus on the Camino. And here, you have to order wine and dessert separately and the portions were not quite as generous. This is when we realized how good we had it while we were walking. Reality was starting to creep in. Wait, I'm not ready…

Day 38 Santiago de Compostela

Reflections

My Facebook post today:

"Good morning from Santiago!

My body's in shock this morning as it was expecting to be walking in hiking boots by now. Instead, I'm still in a warm bed, in a beautiful Airbnb thinking about a cafe con leche later. The only things we have planned today are Mass at noon and laundry. Les promised to cook adobo and rice for dinner.

The enormity of what we accomplished has not sunk in yet but it's safe to say that this was the most difficult thing we've done in our lives.

We're thankful for the support of our friends. Your words of encouragement meant a lot to us. We are especially grateful to those who cheered us on on a daily basis.

What I learned from and loved about this journey:

I knew that Les was a social creature and here, he bloomed. Every time I turned around, he was talking to someone and making them laugh. At the end of the journey, we had so many friends, thanks to him.

Speaking of new friends, oh my goodness, we've had so much fun with them. And more than that, we've had serious conversations as well. It was awesome to get world views on issues important to all men. They're shocked at our gun laws and also couldn't believe that we elected who we did.

Compassion was a big thing on this journey. There were always other pilgrims willing to help, or even just asking if I was ok (the times I was doubled over or gasping for air on the side of a mountain). It was quite nice to see.

We don't need a lot of material things: a couple of shirts, pants, extra undies and a toothbrush is all we really need. Everything else is gravy.

On this trip, it was not nerdy to be religious or spiritual.

We don't know what our bodies are capable of until we test it. Even though I was the slowest walker on the Camino, I kept getting to the next town and the next town and the town after that. Les, by the way, was the second slowest because he kept waiting for me.

• Mishaps will happen: taking the hotel key with you, trying to open the wrong door, losing sunglasses or a t-shirt, getting confused when Google maps tells you to walk on the side of a very busy highway. All these added color to our trip.

When we're walking, we are dead tired and swear that there's no way we could walk the next day. But we get into town, take a hot shower, have vino with our friends, and the next day, miraculously, there's no pain and we're ready to walk again.

• To see the amazing views, you need to climb up a mountain - which is very, very difficult. To have an easy walk, you have to be content with flat ground and boring scenery. I'm sure there's a life lesson there.

• We saw love start and bloom along the way. You see, sometimes love lasts for 30 years, sometimes it lasts for 120 kms and sometimes, 20 kms. However long it lasts, though, love is love so get it where you can.

• Spain oh Spain, you are a beautiful country with equally beautiful people. Your lifestyle is so unique and different from ours that at first it seemed crazy - siestas, late dinners, taking strollers into pubs. But now, I see the beauty of it, the true work/life balance, the focus on family, being flexible. I think I can live here.

True story: one morning, a German couple told the hospitalero: "The church schedule showed that there was supposed to be a pilgrim blessing at 9:30 last night. We went there and there was none." The hospitalero's response: "I guess the priest wasn't around." The Germans looked at me, confused. I shrugged my shoulders and said, "Spain."

We thank the Lord for the successful completion of our journey. Neither of us got sick nor injured, which is a minor miracle in and of itself as we were surrounded by pilgrims who were. If you think about it, one step on a loose stone could have ended our Camino, but it didn't happen.

I think that's it. Please indulge me if I add more later. But for now, we really, really have to do laundry!

Gracias a todos!"

The Cathedral calls us: after we got up this morning, Les and I went to it so we could gaze at it once again. It was very quiet in the plaza mayor. Hardly anyone was walking around in the early hour and I just loved the peacefulness and serenity of the empty square.

We had breakfast afterwards, a cafe con leche and croissant for Les and churros con chocolate for me. The cafe was right next to the building of our flat, which was very convenient. Actually, as I mentioned earlier, there were plenty of restaurants to choose from in old town. There was also a mercado where we planned to go after mass to buy the ingredients for chicken adobo. As it turned out, since today was a Sunday, all the mercados in town were closed so I had to wait another day for my chicken adobo.

We quickly went to the laundromat, also conveniently located around the corner from our flat. The laundromat had interesting decor, with fancy, albeit worn out, tables and chairs. It was authentically shabby chic.

The highlight of the day was Mass at the Cathedral. We went with Myles, Joel and Ross, and I thought we were early but Myles kept telling us to hurry up because once the Cathedral was full, they closed the doors and no one can come in. He was right, because when we got there, the Cathedral was packed and we were the last ones in before they closed the massive doors.

The inside of the Cathedral was awe-inspiring! It had magnificent crystal chandeliers, a big organ and a very high ceiling and looking over us were a lot of arches. The pillars were very big and solid. The inside of the church was cross-shaped, with many rows of pews in front of the altar and a shorter row of pews to its left and right. The altar was magnificent in gold, with angels draped in gold on either side of it. In the middle, above the altar was the famous botafumeiro, or incense burner, that is so big that it takes six to eight men to control the enormous chains that make it swing across the aisles and up, almost to the ceiling of the church. They don't do it for every Mass, and it did not look like they were going to do it for ours.

The Mass was in Spanish, of course, and since it was the noon Mass, it was for the pilgrims. This one was concelebrated by two other priests from different parts of the world. As was customary, the list of countries where the pilgrims who checked into the Cathedral office come from during the last 24 hours was read after the homily. As we expected, a lot came from Spain, but also from Italy, England, the UK and the US. The list was sorted from highest to lowest number of pilgrims so Les and I expected the Philippines to be mentioned last because we identified ourselves as Filipino when we got our compostelas. Alas, the Philippines was not mentioned, having been lumped into the "others" category. We were somewhat disappointed, but it didn't last long.

After Mass, we made our way to the side of the altar where a long line had formed to go up some steps behind the altar so we could embrace the statue of St James from behind. It reminded me so much of Quiapo Church where you can go behind the altar and touch the Nazarene's foot with your handkerchief or veil. Each person had just a few seconds to do this because of the length of the line. I was getting very emotional at this point and started to cry as we got close to our turn. When it was my turn, I gave the statue a quick hug and just thanked God for all the graces He has given me in my life. I did not have time to enumerate what those blessings were because I would have been there a long time. Even now, just writing this, I'm in tears, remembering the feeling of pure joy and gratitude that I felt at that moment.

We went down the steps back to the floor of the church and to the left was a door and past it were steps leading down below the altar, to the tomb of St. James. We were so lucky because there was no one else going down and so we were able to view his tomb by ourselves. The tomb seemed to be in a cave with a glass partition separating us. There was a pew for one person in front of the glass and we had a chance to kneel and pray for about a minute, until there were more people coming down to visit so we left to make room for them. I felt so honored to be able to be in this place and it was so humbling to be in the presence of one who actually walked with the Lord. I told Les this was the closest we'll ever be to Jesus; the man in that tomb walked next to Christ. It doesn't get any closer than that! Les was also awed by the enormity of the moment. This, to me, was the most poignant and significant moment of our Camino.

That afternoon, Les and I went to the train and bus stations to buy tickets to Porto. We wanted to go to Lisbon but they were only selling tickets to Porto so that's what we did. We'll figure out Lisbon later. Since Santiago was in western Spain, and right above Portugal, we decided to go there next.

Walking around town later that day, we saw Luz, who had just arrived, had a drink with her and of course, our three roomies. We were happy to see each other. I'm glad she made it because she was suffering from various aches and pains. Later that night, we had dinner with the guys.

Funny story…early in the Camino, Abby told me that she and the girls had been hanging out with this guy who was married and had four kids. He really wanted to walk the Camino and his wife was so nice that she allowed him to do so. Since Joel was the only guy they were hanging out with at the time, I assumed she was talking about Joel. I told Les about my conversation with Abby. It perplexed us over the course of the Camino that we would see Joel talking and casually flirting with other girls. Les and I concluded that Joel was a nice guy, but a lousy husband. Part of me, though, started to doubt if he was the guy Abby talked about. My doubts were confirmed when we were in Santiago and he said that he was starting to date a girl before he left for Spain and that he hoped that she was waiting for him after he came back. Unfortunately, I didn't have a chance to tell Les about this conversation. At dinner that night, I told Joel about my early conversation with Abby, and how Les and I observed him with the girls on the Camino and how we could not reconcile that Joel with a married Joel. I also told him about my doubts, and about how he confirmed to me earlier in the day that he was not the married man Abby talked about. Well, Joel started laughing so hard, and at the same time, Les looked at me very strangely, because it was the first time he heard that Joel was not the married man we thought he was. It took a while for that to sink in. In the meantime, Joel, Myles and Ross were laughing hysterically, and Les and I joined in. I'm sure that Joel still laughs to himself whenever he thinks of this evening and our conversation. In our subsequent conversations on social media, I make sure to always ask Joel about his nonexistent wife and four kids.

Day 39 Santiago de Compostela

Rejoicing

The grocery stores are open - yeay!!! We bought ingredients for chicken adobo and lugaw (soup with rice, ginger, garlic and chicken). The grocery store literally had one bottle of soy sauce, only one size (small) and believe me, we used every last drop of it.

Our roommates really liked the food but did not eat much because they (well, all of us) were eating out and partying; still celebrating because we were still in such a state of euphoria.

Ross left today, but not before seeing his erstwhile Camino romance Berni, who was taking over his spot in the AirBnb. I was sad to see Ross leave.

When we were at the AirBnb, Joel was singing one of his compositions to Berni and Les just burst into the room to ask him a question. Myles and I laughed our heads off. Not that Joel was trying to make the moves on Berni, but my husband's total lack of timing is so funny. We just laughed a lot in our four days in Santiago.

Day 40 Finisterre

The End of the Camino (in Spain)

Today's Facebook post:

"After two days of decompression in Santiago, today we headed to Finisterre, also called Fisterra, which is at the end of a peninsula, surrounded on three sides by water. During biblical times, people thought that it was literally the end of the world - hence the name.

When St. James was sent to the ends of the earth to preach the gospel, this is where he went so it's an important site for pilgrims. Some of our friends walked another four days to get here, some biked, and we took the bus but walked the three kms from the town to the marker.

The 0.00 marker indicates that it's the true end of the Camino. I'm so glad we came here because we couldn't have picked a more beautiful day to officially close our Camino. This day marks the end of our Camino."

As we were walking back from the zero kilometer marker to town, we saw a man biking, or rather, walking his bike uphill to the same marker. Les recognized him as Jim, or "SoCal" as we referred to him as he was from Southern California. After we said our hellos, I told him that it was just two more kms and I thought that would make him happy knowing that it was so close, but instead, he was bummed because he was tired and running on fumes. In addition, he was trying to make it back to town to take the 3 PM bus back to Santiago. We told him we were going to be on the same bus.

We got back to town and looked for a place to eat that had a view of the bus stop. The first restaurant we went to was closed and the second one had owners who spoke German, which was great for the Germans pilgrims, I guess. We ordered our food and the owner waited on us and he asked us where we were from. We gave our usual answer of "originally from the Philippines but now living in San Francisco." He got so excited because he was in San Francisco in the 70s and he went off to get his photo album. In the meantime, who shows up but Steffen, the German, who we were very happy to see. We did our huggy-huggies and he asked me about Luz and before I could say anything, Les said she's coming to Finisterra with Bernie on a bus later today. He was absolutely thrilled but nervous to hear that and he asked us if he should meet her or not. I told him he probably should, for closure. They were an item for about 100 kms on the Camino and he wrote "te amo Luz" on at least 100 rocks along the way and at least ten road signs. Steffen was very conflicted but in the end, when we rode the bus back, he was on the bench at the bus stop. In later days, we would see his social media posts with very artistic pictures of him, Luz and Berni having a good time in Finisterre.

Anyway, as we were having this conversation, SoCal Jim showed up, terribly hungry, and ordered food from the same man who had been to San Francisco. The man took his order, disappeared, and came back with his photo albums of 70s pictures of San Francisco. The pictures were old and faded and the city did not look like today's SF, but the man's memory was still very sharp and he was telling us what was happening in the pictures, taking his time regaling us with his memories. Jim was going crazy with hunger and the fact that the bus was arriving in 20 minutes and he didn't want to miss it. At the same time, Steffen was trying to have a heart to heart talk with me about Luz. It was so chaotic, with each of us having separate conversations.

I think Jim finally got through to the man about how little time we had and he got his food. He ordered a salad (which turned out to be a big one) and another dish, which I can't remember now. Between his hunger and his panic of being left by the bus, he started eating really fast, and apologizing to us that he was not eating properly. He said that if his wife Inez had been there, she would have slapped him for being so improper. We didn't have a problem with it,

but we just learned that Jim was a very proper person.

We all made the bus back, bike and all. Jim started telling us a little bit of stories about his work, with NBC I believe, and he told us that he had just retired. We had seen Jim intermittently on the Camino and it was the first time we talked about what he used to do. I guess we were all mentally preparing for our return to real life, as we had been living in this bubble that's the Camino for the past five weeks or so.

Jim also told us that he and his friends John and Don were going out to dinner that night and asked if we wanted to join them. I told him that instead of doing that, they should just come over to the flat for chicken adobo fried rice and lugaw. He asked if the two other guys could come too and we said sure, because I think we had enough food for a lot of people. He promised to take care of the wine and we decided on a time.

Apparently, Joel and Myles also asked Lucy, the British singer, to stay in the flat tonight (Berni left today), and Virginija (the Lithuanian who now lives in London) and her friend Jason (from the US) were also coming over for dinner. Instant party!

Everyone really liked the food, and for most of them, it was their first time trying Filipino food. It made Les and me feel like ambassadors of Filipino food to the world. I told Jim that I was really surprised that he never had Filipino food as he lived in SoCal, and he said that in his neighborhood, ethnic food meant Italian. Les teased him, where do you live? Malibu? Bingo! Les and I would later meet with Jim and his stunning wife Inez in Malibu, walk around his 'hood and have an al fresco lunch in his beautiful garden. His house subsequently burned down in the big fire of 2018 which made Les and me very sad. It made our visit with him all the more poignant. And I digress one last time…

The get-together that evening was very meaningful, and Lucy performed a couple of songs that she composed and Joel sang his compositions as well. Lucy walked with her guitar the whole way and Joel brought his guitar/not guitar with him. We went around the room and shared our insights as to what surprised us the most about the Camino, and all sorts of meaningful things. John was a pleasant surprise that night. When we saw him on the way, he hardly talked except that one time when he asked us to root for the Dodgers in the World Series. John was very chatty that night, which was great. We learned that he was a lawyer who did not take the bar until 20 years after he graduated - and he passed! I thought it was impressive but he said his family did not seem to think so. Ah, family. John worked at the LA Times for years. I told him about our daughter Asia going to law school the next school year and he told me to keep him posted on her progress. John was such a revelation that night. Inez later told us that that was the real John. Quiet John was a mystery to her.

Myles left that night. It was very bittersweet because the goodbyes were coming before I was ready. I got so used to being around these three guys and they were just disappearing one by one. I guess life doesn't wait until you're ready for change. It just happens. I'll miss these three guys the most.

After dinner, Jim treated us all to ice cream. As it happened, there was an ice cream shop next door (I love this neighborhood!) so we all went down there, had ice cream and coffee, and said our good-byes. The kids went off to find night-time entertainment, the adults went home to rest and Les and I cleaned up the kitchen and prepared for our early train ride to Porto. The next morning, I was so sad because I didn't want to leave yet. And yet, I was ready for our next adventure, the cities we were about to visit and our first ever cruise at the end of

our trip. I was ready for the 800th km, I was ready for the rest of my life.

Thus our day ended. Thus a chapter of our lives ended. But no, it didn't really end. We now have friends for life, with our shared experiences and story-telling. Now I know why people do the Camino more than once because man, I can't wait to get back and do it all over again!

I don't know if I've changed or how I've changed. I guess we'll find out once I get back to real life. I hope I'm now a better person. It was easy to be a good person on the Camino because most everyone was. It's what comes after that will be a challenge. I am encouraged by what Steffen told me when I confided in him that I was worried about backsliding into old habits and ways of thinking. He told me that backsliding will indeed happen, but when it does, it will feel uncomfortable so you have no option but to go back to the ways of the Camino. With these words and God's help, I believe that we were now truly on the right path.

THE END (of our first Camino) :)

Epilogue: Two Years Later

It's been two years since we came back from Spain. After the Camino, we had time to visit several cities before going on a cruise that was meant to be our R&R from walking so much. The switch from pilgrim to tourist was jarring and I feel like we missed the chance for the introspection that should have happened at the end of the Camino. Nonetheless, here are some insights that I've gleamed since coming back:

- Nothing totally prepares you for the Camino. All the practice hikes, all the decisions and the minutiae of which sleeping bag to buy or what socks to wear: it's all just stuff. While it certainly helps to be physically and materially prepared for it, you also have to be spiritually prepared, and in the right mental state. We were very lucky that the hospitalero in Saint Jean Pied de Port, our starting point, gave us a short lecture of how we should be open to everyone we meet, as God will send each of them to us to teach us something specific.
- The Camino is a miraculous place. Every night, as Les and I stumbled into our albergue or hostel, our feet ached, our bodies ached and we were never sure if we could do it all over again the next day. But every morning, we woke up refreshed and raring to go, with no more pain. Les brought a bagful of Motrin thinking that he would need all of it, but we both used it sparingly, only in extreme fatigue and pain.
- The noise of the outside world was a reality that marred my Camino. I didn't want to focus on it a lot in my daily journal of events, but during a big part of the Camino, I was extremely stressed about some retirement issues back home that I was trying to resolve from Spain. There were days when I was in tears thinking about it. Obviously, everything worked out in the end, as Les kept telling me it would - and I should have believed him. While it is ideal to leave all your cares behind, it's not always possible. And while I'm on this subject, I can't thank my daughter Isabella enough for helping me resolve this issue.
- The opportunity for prayer and introspection (on things other than the bullet point above) was endless and I took full advantage. Les always walked a ways in front of me so I was able to repeatedly pray the rosary and just talk to God. I honestly thought it was the closest that I had to a direct line to God. You can say coincidence, and I say it was divine intervention that after a few days of prayer and lighting candles at every church we went

into, we received a text from our younger daughter Asia telling us that she got a good LSAT score, exactly what I was praying for.

• The Camino is a bubble and in that bubble are really nice people. We noticed that pretty much everyone on the trail was very spiritual and looking for answers to profound questions. Some had gotten laid off, or divorced, or at some crossroads of life (only my husband said that he was doing it because I wanted to; he did not want to stay home alone). It seemed to me as if we were all there to help each other, if only by listening or sharing a meal. Because we were surrounded by good people, we took that with us when we left the bubble to go back home. Back-sliding is a reality, but as a wise pilgrim said, if you go back to your old ways, it will feel uncomfortable and you will right yourself. And he was right!

• It's been two years since we've come back, but we still have conversations with our friends who followed our journey through social media about how much they enjoyed it and how it affected them. Several have told us that they couldn't wait to read about what we had done that day and because of the time difference, my entry for each day was available as our friends in the US were waking up. We had no idea about all this, because they waited until they saw us in person to tell us. It's very heart-warming!

Since returning from Spain, Les and I have become more active in church, volunteering for different things. I think that service to others is what I need to do in the second act of my life. I've done half a lifetime chasing the paper, as the kids say. Our first-hand experience of being helped on the Camino, all the angels who were there for us, that's the kind of person I want to be.

My completion of the Camino, and its many physical challenges, has given me a new perspective of myself. I did it! I got my swagger back. Now I feel like because I did it, I can do anything.

Les and I are now both happily retired and content, loving the time we spend with our children and grandchildren. We've gotten past a sticking point in our marriage, something that has caused our worst arguments (which are actually few and far-between but annoying nonetheless) and I couldn't be happier. The journey to a better me has started and will not end any time soon (there's a lot to fix!). Les and I still talk to people about the magic of the Camino every chance we get and I suspect that my daily feed on social media influenced a few friends to go on it as well. Best of all, we are in touch with the friends we made on the trails and talking to them brings back all the wonderful feelings we had while we were together. A big thank you to all of them for being there when we were on our journey. God sent us exactly the right people to meet. May God bless you all!

Appendix 1 Help Along the Way

It is impossible to go on the Camino, much less finish it, without the help of the shell and arrow symbols on the trail as well as the free water refill stations in every town. The yellow and blue shell and arrow symbols told us which way to go and ran the gamut from tiles on the pavement, to a swath of yellow paint on tree trunks to stone formations. Each of the shell rays denotes a different Camino starting point and all the rays meet in a place called Santiago de Compostela. The water stations which sustained us physically and helped us financially, ranged from simple to elaborate but always provided, as the Camino always does.

Appendix 2. Pilgrim Meals

We learned that in Spain, restaurants were required to provide a daily economical option on their menu. It was called the "menu del dia" and on the Camino, it was known as the Pilgrim Menu. Typically 10 euros, it included bread, a primero plato of either a salad, noodles, or paella and a segundo plato of fried pork, bacalao, callos or beef stew, *always* with French fries, dessert of flan, yogurt, fruit or ice cream and wine (for two people, it was usually a bottle). The vast majority of the meals were delicious and all of them were plentiful. Dessert could be funny: Joel ordered the fruit and he got an apple on a dessert plate to be eaten with a fork and knife. I once ordered ice cream and got a wrapped ice cream bar on a dessert plate. Some days we would simply buy bread, cold cuts and cheese for lunch on the road or dinner in our room. Breakfast was usually a torta de patata, or croissant, cafe con leche and orange juice. Happy hour was happiest with pintxos, tapas, olives, gherkins and cocktail onions. And of course, my favorite snack was churros con chocolate.

Appendix 3. In Memoriam

We were made very aware early on that there were pilgrims who did not finish their Caminos because they died along the way. From what we heard, some died from physical reasons like heart attacks and dehydration, some from weather-related reasons like heavy mountain fog causing falls and some from vehicle-related accidents. We passed more than fifty crosses and tombstones marking the places where these pilgrims fell. We were lucky that we did not come close to serious injury and we honor those who were not as fortunate.

Bibliography

Brierley, John, A Pilgrim's Guide to the Camino de Santiago Camino Frances St. Jean Pied de Port - Santiago de Compostela. Scotland: CAMINO GUIDES, 2018.

The Way. Dir Emilio Estevez. Elixir Films, 2010. Film

I'll Push You. Emota Inc, 2017. DVD

Acknowledgements

Thank you to everyone who helped me complete this project!

A big thank you to my editor Jan Quilici, who was the first non-Camino person who read and edited my manuscript and told me that it was a "wonderful book that needed to be written." Her early validation was very important to me.

To the pilgrims whose stories I weaved in with ours. You guys have been so supportive especially during times when the task at hand was overwhelming. Your positive responses had overwhelmed me as well! Thank goodness we met the nicest and the most interesting people on our Camino; otherwise, this book would have been so boring. You guys are all so special to us and I will not name you in this section because I've already named all of you in the book. Special thanks to SoCal Jim, though, for taking the time to write the description in the back cover of this book.

To my husband, who read up to page 17 of the manuscript, and who will probably never get to the end of this book. Maybe I need to come up with an audio book version that he can listen to while he rides his bike so he'll know how it ends. He has been my greatest supporter nonetheless, and plied me with food and coffee when I was writing this.

To those who read my daily social media posts while we were on the Camino and said, "you should write a book!" Well, here it is!

Made in the USA
Monee, IL
31 October 2019

16119498R00081